BUILDING YOUR BRAND

BUILDING YOUR BRAND

A BEGINNER'S GUIDE TO STARTING YOUR SMALL BUSINESS

LUVELL STEPTER

F.L.A.M.E Publishing

F.L.A.M.E Publishing
www.flameproductions.com
info@flameproductions.com
Cover design: F.L.A.M.E Graphic Design

For information about special discounts available for bulk purchases, sales promotions, fund-raising and educational needs, contact F.L.A.M.E Productions Sales at 1-203.772.8996 or sales@flameproductions.com.

Printed in the United States of America
First Printing, 2016
ISBN 978-1-329-94520-3
ISBN 978-1-329-95623 (Hardcover)

First Edition
14 13 12 11 10 / 10 9 8 7 6 5 4 3 2 1

This book is dedicated to:

My wife Karla, and our newborn son
Noah.

All I do is for you both.

Foreword

I have often been asked about how I started my business. Many have asked "What were some of the tools and methods used to get things started?". So, after countless phone calls, DM's and emails, I decided to write a guide full of the tools and resources that I have gathered throughout the years.

I have spent over 10,000 hours researching and gathering information, as well as numerous nights going to bed at 4 a.m., studying facts and data to help fulfill my dreams. It is my pleasure to help a new entrepreneur save time and headaches by helping you through this difficult, but rewarding journey. I have gathered large amounts of vital data to help you achieve your goals and have compiled that information into this book. Included in this guide are links and pictures of significant information to assist you in your journey.

Most of the knowledge gained in this guide came through reading, coupled with much trial and error. To be a successful entrepreneur, you (and I emphasize the YOU) must be a reader.

There is no escaping it. Even if you find information from a valuable contact or resource, you must do the research to check out its validity and then apply it strategically to your business. It is my goal through this book to encourage you to succeed in your business. Whether it's in fashion or not, this book will give you the foundational stones to get started with building your company and brand. Take note: After reading and processing the information in this guide, remember nothing happens without action! You must apply it to see it manifest.

Lavell Spotter

CONTENTS

PUBLISHING

ACKNOWLEDGMENT

FOREWORD

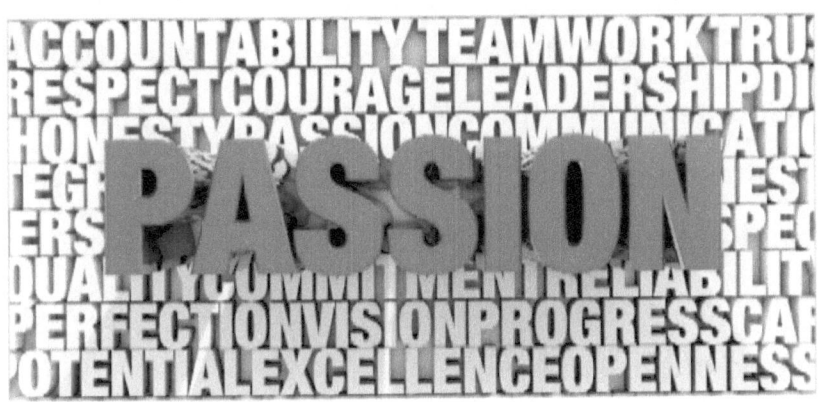

Chapter 1

What is your passion?

Many times I ask people, "What is your passion?" With that loaded question, I have received a variety of answers from design to daycare, music to computer repair and the list goes on and on.

The reason I ask this question is to see if people are really living out their dreams or are still dreaming about them. I believe each person has a passion and a talent to do something. There is a gift or talent inside of you that the world is waiting on to make it better than it was before.

Before starting a business, this question should be answered. You do not want to waste years of your life, time and money on an expensive hobby. When deciding what you should do for your business, it should always be connected with your passion. Starting a business solely to make money won't last long at all. In the many cycles and learning curves of business, you will need a strong passion to take you through the highs and lows of business ownership.

I just don't know

Many people know they are not meant to work all of their lives to make someone else rich by fulfilling another person's dream. Most people are just unaware of where their passion lies. Sometimes, it's right in front of your face, while at other times you may need to search it out. Discovering what you're passionate about can help you find out what you will contribute to the world.

For those of you who don't know, here is a quick list of questions to help you narrow down what your passion may be:

- What are you good at doing?

- What would you do even if you didn't get paid to do it?

- What subject do you know the most about?

- What subject gets you fired up when you hear someone mentioning it?

- Are you good with your hands?

- Are you creative?

- Have people told you they would buy your product if you were selling it?

- Does a certain skill or talent come easy to you?

- Do you always think about this skill or talent?

- Have several people suggested that this skill is something you should be doing?

If you are able to answer some of the above questions, it can be a good start on pinpointing what you are meant to do. People often get discouraged because their gift or talent is not one that can be seen by the masses, but you must realize your offering to the world is no less important. Just consider your body for instance. Some of your most important parts are on the inside of you and without them you wouldn't be alive! In most cases, they are not seen at all, but it does not take away from their importance. Recognize your gift and accept it. Become the best that you can at it.

After narrowing down the questions you have answered from the above list, find a field that is already connected to your passion and reinvent it or become the best at it. Your gift is most likely connected to helping someone else in some shape or form. Your job is to dig it out and learn more about it to enhance your skill-set.

Adding Value

You add value to your talent or skill by studying it. The more you know, the more you can grow in your field. When you become proficient in your area of expertise you can help others. By adding more knowledge and increasing your skills in your passion, you also add value to your life and your pocket book. People get paid for the value of the knowledge they bring to a company. A company's worth is only as valuable as its employees and the knowledge they bring to the table.

Take as many classes as you can. Read as many books as you can. Ask questions. Research daily and inquire about your passion and gift. Find out what makes it work as well as fail. Learn who has become successful doing it and what are some of the things they did to become successful.

The more valuable you become, the more of an asset you are to the world and those who are in need of your gift, service or product. Your passion is the answer to someone's question. Your skill-set can add value to many people's lives.

Learn from every possible source. Once you have recognized your passion and honed your craft, now it's time to get to work.

BRAND BUILDING QUOTE:

MY MISSION IN LIFE IS NOT MERELY TO SURVIVE, BUT TO THRIVE; AND TO DO SO WITH SOME PASSION, SOME COMPASSION, SOME HUMOR, AND SOME STYLE.

MAYA ANGELOU

Never work a day in your life!

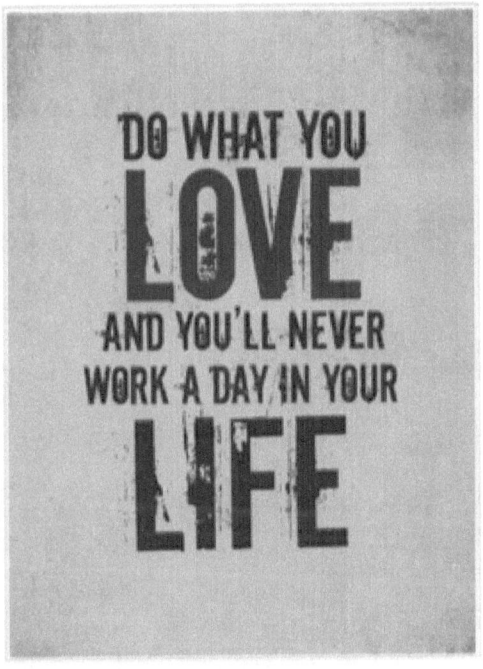

DO WHAT YOU LOVE AND YOU'LL NEVER WORK A DAY IN YOUR LIFE

We have all heard the saying, "Find a job that you love and you will never work a day in your life." This saying is true, if you are passionate about what you are doing. To you, the ups and downs of a hard workday are mere stepping stones to your mountain of success. The reason it doesn't seem like work is because it comes natural to you. It's unrealistic to believe you won't have hard days because they will come. Nothing comes easy to anyone trying to climb the success ladder.

Nothing Comes Easy

In reality, it will take hard work to bring yourself your brand and your company to the place that you have only seen in your dreams. Success is not for the faint at heart. It will make you work, sweat and cry before it yields you its fruits of rewards. Nothing that comes easy will have the sustaining power to last.

Building your brand will not be an easy task. For many months and even years, you will be the first in the office and the last to leave. You will be the CEO, the secretary, the janitor and the accountant. These are great steps to learn on the ground floor before handing them off to someone else. Reading and listening to others' trials and errors will become your best friend. Nothing teaches you a better lesson than going out and learning from your own mistakes.

There will be times when you want to give up. There will be times when you will wonder if you are in the right business, BUT take heart, this is when your passion will kick into full gear. It enforces the notion that nothing will stop you from being successful.

Passion coupled with action is so important that it weeds out billionaires from dreamers. Your true passion will not let you quit when the going gets tough. It will consistently think of ways to overcome all adversity. Passion never takes "NO" for an answer. It knows someway or somehow there is a way to get a "YES", and it will find it. Although nothing will come easy, it is your passion that will encourage you and let you know that it will all be worth it.

Discovering your passion and purpose coupled with persistence will distance you from anyone who started a business just to make money. Your passion will sustain you when the down times come. It will uplift you when you see your purpose manifested. It will encourage you when you want to give up. It will catapult you over any obstacle.

You are no different from many inventors and business owners who found their passion and are now living their dream. You are capable of producing the same result. Knowing and living your passion and purpose is one of the greatest "ah-ha" moments in life. When you realize your gift, it can elevate someone's life and perhaps change the world.

BRAND BUILDING FACT:

SMALL BUSINESSES EMPLOY 57% OF THE COUNTRY'S PRIVATE WORKFORCE

Chapter 2

So you want to start a brand?

One of the best decisions you can make is going into business for yourself. Having the independence of exploring and living your dreams is second to none. Having the power to change the world or make a difference in the lives of others cannot be truly measured until you see your dream unfold. There are countless rewards and benefits to starting your own business.

Before you can reap these rewards, there are inevitable questions the budding entrepreneur must ask and eventually answer. Where do you start? How do you start? How much money do you need to start? To the budding entrepreneur these are inevitable questions that must be answered. Step-by-step we will go through your initial "aha" moments in starting a business and the process of acquiring the tools and resources you need to build your business and brand.

What is a brand?

Image courtesy of Branding Strategy Insider

A brand is defined as a "a class of goods identified by a name as the product of a single firm or manufacturer; a characteristic or distinctive kind." We are surrounded by and exposed to brands constantly, sometimes without even noticing it. They appear in our music, television shows and ads, even the tags on our clothes. Because our minds are constantly being flooded with the advertisements of brands, deposits are being made into our subconscious without us knowing it. That brand deposit is then regurgitated when it's time to fulfill a certain need or want, causing us to build faith, trust, and belief in certain products. These deposits also cause us to see brands as a personal representation of ourselves. Which brings us to the question... What is your brand?

You have a Personal Brand

Since the time you were born you have been creating your personal brand; from the products you buy, to the music you listen to, and the places you shop. All of these intricate pieces of you build up your personal brand. When people look at you, they expect certain things from your character because of the personal brand that you have constructed over the years, whether it is positive or negative. Many of the gifts we receive are based on how someone views your personal brand. As you begin to create the brand for your business, think about your brand as a living organism. It is a representation of your products, services and expertise.

Here are a couple of questions to ask yourself as you prepare to build your brand. Write these questions and the answers down for future reference.

BRAND BUILDING FACT:

80% OF CONSUMERS SAID "AUTHENTICITY OF CONTENT" IS THE MOST INFLUENTIAL FACTOR IN THEIR DECISION TO BECOME A FOLLOWER OF A BRAND.

What is YOUR brand?

- What is my brand? Is it hip, cool, serious, funny, child-oriented, etc.

- What does my brand stand for?

- Am I a personal reflection of my brand? (when people see it will they think of me)?

- Will it be a common use brand or luxury brand?

- Will it serve as a symbol of hope?

- How will my brand evolve over the course of time?

- Do I need to bring in other people (celebrities, community leaders, established companies, etc.) to validate my brand?

- Can my brand be confused with another brand?

- What makes my brand different?

- What will draw people to my brand?

- Who will be attracted to this brand?

As you begin on the ground floor with building your brand and business, remember that your brand is a representation of your company and core values. In this beginning stage of your brand building, decide in what way you want your brand to be represented to the world. Imagine your customer base, how does your ideal customer look? How do you see your customers interacting with your brand? Build your brand around your core values for what you do as a company and the services your provide. Your brand should always be consistent wherever it appears. Take your brand seriously.

Think about your marketing. How will you present your brand to the world? What products or services are you going to offer that have not been done before?

Learn who your customer is. Learn about what they do and don't like. What are their shopping habits with exposable income? Where do they like to shop? How much do they spend on average? These are some of the questions you should consider while building your brand, creating your price points and structuring your product to suit your consumers.

BRAND BUILDING FACT:
76% OF CONSUMERS SAY THEY VIEW CUSTOMER SERVICE AS THE TRUE TEST OF HOW MUCH A COMPANY VALUES THEM.

(2015 ASPECT CONSUMER EXPERIENCE SURVEY)

What's in a Name?

Your name selection is of great importance. Your name should have meaning. It can be something you are most passionate about: a person that has left a great impression in your life; or a word that embodies the core foundation of your company's values.

Many businesses take on the character of their business names. Be careful not to name your company something that could be extremely hard to pronounce, cause confusion with another brand or could mean something totally different in another language. A good name rolls smooth off the tongue. It is easy to remember, and sometimes it can be connected with a well known object to trigger customers memories. Some names are easy to build themes around; themes for your website, product, store or logo which we will discuss in the next chapter.

Think carefully about your business name. This will be the first words that will be uttered by you or others when describing or mentioning your brand. Let it be memorable, catchy, and a great representation of your company and brand.

Your Niche

What is a niche? A niche is a distinct segment of a market. It is what makes you different from the rest. What is your niche? What can you and will you do to make your business different? Many successful entrepreneurs either find a new niche or define an old niche with new thinking or a new product. Think about some things that you can do to make your brand stand out from the rest.

YOUR LOGO

Your logo may be the first interaction your customers have with you and your brand. Next to your service or product, your logo will be one of the most recognizable things about your company and brand. Your logo should be a great representation of your company. If you have a luxury brand your logo should reflect it. No matter what your genre of business is, your logo should mirror what you are all about.

When creating your logo there are a few things that should be considered before designing or having your logo designed for you.

- Your logo should be a strong representation of your business.

- You should seek a professional to design your logo.

- Your logo should not be busy with a lot of text and pictures.

- Decide if you want a text logo, graphic logo, image logo, or a combination of those various forms.

- Your logo should be easy to read.

- Your logo should be easy to understand the business it represents. (If you are selling homes or cars you don't need to put them in your logo.)

- Your logo should be able to work in multiple formats: color, black and white, greyscale.

- Your logo should draw your target audience.

- Can your logo cause consumer confusing with an existing logo?

- What will make your logo different?

- What is my company/Brand tagline? (Should I add it in my logo?)

- What color or colors will I use for my logo?

- What emotions or feeling do I want my logo to evoke?

- Is my logo pleasing to the eye?

You may have a favorite color but that does not mean it should show up in your logo, unless it effectively represents your business. Remember, colors can elicit an emotional reaction from your targeted audience. Brands often use different colors or themes to garner specific emotions. These are some of the things you should consider when creating your brand.

Image courtesy of zohardesigns

Take a look at what some of the more commonly used colors can signify:

- **Blue**: Trust, dependability, and strength.

- **Red**: Action and energy; can elicit a passionate response, but also aggression.

- **Yellow**: Optimism, positivity, motivation, warmth.

- **Green**: Nature and serenity. Can imply good health. Lighter greens = more peaceful. Deeper greens signify wealth or prestige.

- **Purple**: Creativity, mysterious, sophisticated.

- **Orange**: Energy, friendliness, confidence.

- **Pink**: Femininity, excitement, romance, and youthfulness. Light pink has sentimental tones, hot pink has high energy.

- **Brown**: Dependability, simplicity. Associated with nature, strength.

It's advised to stick to no more than three colors in your logo and to always look at it in one, two, and three-color options.

If you're wondering how you might stack up to the world's top brands when it comes to logo type and color usage, check out these stats below from (TCreative)

- 33% use blue

- 29% use red

- 28% use black or gray scale

- 13% use yellow or gold

- 95% use only one or two colors

- 41% use text only

- 9% don't feature the company name at all

- 5% use more than two colors

An effective logo is **distinctive, appropriate, practical, graphic, simple in form** and conveys an intended message. In its simplest form, a logo identifies but to do this effectively it must follow the basic principles of logo design:

- **A logo must be simple.** A simple logo allows for easy recognition and allows the logo to be versatile and memorable. Effective logos feature something unexpected or unique without being overdrawn.

- **A logo must be memorable.** Following closely behind the principle of simplicity is that of memorability. An effective logo should be memorable and this is achieved by having a simple yet appropriate logo. (Think of McDonald's golden arches on a red background.)

• **A logo must be enduring.** An effective logo should endure the test of time. The logo should be 'future proof', meaning that it should still be effective in 10, 20, 50+ years time.

• **A logo must be versatile.** An effective logo should be able to work across a variety of mediums and applications.

• **A logo must be appropriate.** How you position the logo should be appropriate for its intended purpose. For a more detailed explanation see: What makes a good logo? http://just-creative.com/2009/07/27/what-makes-a-good-logo/

As you can see, creating a brand and logo is no simple task. Having a strong brand is vital in achieving success. For example look at past presidential races and you can see many of the candidates branding themselves with their own personal logos or building their brand from their experiences.

Consider these things before bringing your product to market. Having an idea in your head is fine but, evolving that idea to manifest into a brand requires hard work and numerous failures. Don't be afraid to fail. Failure is actually in the formula of success. We will go over that in more detail in a later chapter.

For more information on logos and logo design, check out these websites.

http://www.creativebloq.com/graphic-design/pro-guide-logo-design-21221

http://logodesignerblog.com/logo-design-tips-you-can-learn-from-the-worlds-biggest-brands/

IF YOU BUILD IT THEY WILL COME.

This quote cannot be farther from the truth. Many people, including myself thought, "When I get this business started, I am going to need hundreds of suitcases just to hold all the money." This is not always reality. Not to say that your business will not be successful, but don't let your expectations exceed your current reality. When I started my own business, I realized that my mind and my current situation then painted two different pictures. Neither one of them were wrong, but at some point the two must come together as one cohesive reality. Initially, we often think, "As long as my product is launched and in the marketplace, the money will come in great abundance." We can just picture ourselves with plenty of money rolling in and so many orders that we don't know what to do with ourselves (see image below).

Eventually the honeymoon phase is over and reality sets in. Your family and friends are no longer so supportive and now you are forced to market your brand and persuade the world to consume your product. We look and feel like this.

The Formula

After you discover that the preconceived notions you had about having your own business are not reality, don't panic. Now is the time to find the formula that works best for your business and the process in making each part come together for your brand. Review the chart below for brand building. We will go over each step in further detail.

1.The Idea Stages of Brand Building

It is in this stage when the ideas are flowing fresh in your mind. You have a vision, plan and purpose for your company or brand. You have done your homework and hours of research, you are now ready to launch out into the deep. You ask for family and friends support and everyone is jumping on the bandwagon. You are told this is the best idea since sliced bread. All the enthusiasm is so thick you would need a samurai sword to cut it. So, you start your business and things are going well, sells are coming in and you have 80 or so likes on your Facebook page. Family and friends are walking billboards for you. Business is great! If you knew it would have started off this great, you would have done it years ago. Soon you start to contemplate how and when you will quit your job, because you will soon be raking in millions of dollars, while your old working buddies sit in the office and contemplate their life's decisions (sound familiar). You are now building your proof of concept.

Proof of Concept

What is proof of concept? A proof of concept (POC) or a proof of principle is a realization of a certain method or idea to demonstrate its feasibility, or a demonstration in principle, whose purpose is to verify that some concept or theory has the potential of being used.

In the business world, POC is how startups demonstrate that a product is financially viable. POC involves extensive research and review and is submitted as a single package to concerned parties. It includes examination of the revenue model, in which companies show projected revenue from products and services, and indicate development cost, long-term finance projections and how much the service costs to maintain and market. It's an excellent way for a business to evaluate itself internally and at proposed acquisitions and projects.

To put it simply. Establishing proof of concept is you introducing your product to the market to see if there is a viable need for your product or business accompanied by sales in some cases.

While going through this critical stage of growth and excitement, it is important that you should not get ahead of yourself. A great piece of advice is to take every compliment with a grain of salt and every criticism as an opportunity for growth. In this stage you should see what is and isn't working for you. Learn what you can do to improve what isn't working. The things that work, will continue to take care of themselves, but if you neglect your weak points you will create self-inflicted headaches.

At this stage, you should already know what your profit margins are, who your targeted customers are and where you plan to sell your products or service. It is to be hoped that at this point you have already talked to a store manager and shown them samples of your planned work. If nothing else, you should have a game plan to get your product into the hands of your consumers. Enjoy this stage, this is your baby taking its first steps. We all know that with the first steps comes, the first fall.

BRAND BUILDING FACT:

48% OF AMERICANS EXPECT BRANDS TO KNOW THEM AND HELP THEM DISCOVER NEW PRODUCTS OR SERVICES THAT FIT THEIR NEEDS.

2. The Passion Stages

Your baby has now taken off. When people see you, they may even associate you with your brand. You may be introduced to others in this regard, "Hey here is my friend _____ and they have this brand..." Everything has been rolling smooth until now, you have a few sales and your name is really getting out there. What people don't see is that your business is literally hanging from a thread. If you don't make another sale soon, your business will eventually be a mere venture that you did at some point in your life. It is at this critical stage, when you come to the realization of, if you are in this for the long run or, was this just a quick hobby that you needed to get out of your system.

What do you do when the money no longer flows like it did in the beginning and your customers try to avoid you for fear of being badgered with a sales pitch to buy your product?

What do you do when you are running out of money and can only make it a few weeks with what you have saved? What do you do when you have placed a large order with your manufacturer and the order comes back all wrong?

Talk to any entrepreneur that has had any level of success, they will tell you that we all have been at this stage. This is the stage where you don't give up! This is the stage when you discover your amount of determination. Do you really want to succeed regardless of all the No's that you have encountered in the past few weeks or months? Do you really want to succeed even though you can't see how you are going to get out of your current business crisis?

Success will not let you succeed until you have paid the ultimate price of hard work and due diligence in your particular field. These are your dues and the rights of passage to the next level. It is in these trying times that you will see what your business and you are made of. During this time, it would be a great time to reconstruct or change some of the weaknesses in your business. This could be the virus that has slowed down your sales. The problem also could be you. Have you lost the enthusiasm you once had now that all the fanfare and hoopla has died down? NO ONE, NO ONE, will care or treat your business better than you do. You are where the buck stops and starts. You are the creator extraordinaire, and your business' lifeline depends on you getting past this point.

Your passion should be so strong at this stage for your business that whatever failure you have received you turn it into fuel and use it to ignite your passion and overcome your current obstacles.

The feeling of giving up sometimes comes with this process, it is this make or break moment that life throws at you, to see if you are all in. Whenever I am faced with a difficult slump in my business, I often think of myself as the guy at the top of this picture (see picture below). I am a self-proclaimed optimist. My passion tells me I am one moment away from my ideas changing the world. You will need this type of thinking and passion to get you to the next stage.

NEVER STOP TRYING

You never know how close you are to your Destiny.
Luvell Stepter

3. The Value Stage

Because you didn't give up like many before you and have weathered the storm, you are now in what I like to call the value stage. You have gained incredible and valuable insight in what it takes to see your business through a dive. Hopefully, you have started devising plans to revitalize your business. Your mistakes and previous failures have given you vital information on what to do and what not to do.

This is a good time to get a mentor. Find someone who is already in the field that you are in. Reach out to them and let them know that you are interested in picking their brain. Because you have endured a difficult time with your company and brand they may even put you under their wing after seeing your tenacity.

These mentors may be extremely busy. They may not have much time to give you so try taking them out to lunch or dinner. Do whatever you can to make this connection. The value they have obtained and experience garnered through their businesses life cycle is invaluable information. If your mentor or the people that you are interested in having as your mentor are not within your reach, no worries! You have all the information that you need at your fingertips thanks to Google, YouTube and your local library or bookstore. I have plenty of mentors who don't even know that they are my mentors. I also have mentors who have huge names in the entertainment and business industries with whom I have had the pleasure of meeting and having informative personal private sessions. The information obtained in these encounters has saved me an inordinate amount of time and unnecessary stress. There are other mentors whom I learn from afar. I have purchased their books and CDs and learned from their mistakes. A good mentor to have in your arsenal is Jim Rohn. One of my mentors introduced me to Jim Rohn by way of one of his CDs and my life catapulted to a higher level. I recommend getting your hands on any of his materials.

Here is some great information on finding a mentor in your industry. This site has online courses on various business skills that you can take for free! http://www.skilledup.com/articles/how-to-find-a-mentor-to-take-your-skills-to-the-next-level

The value stage is where you want to grow your business. Advertise, expand try a different color, try a different approach. Spend as much time as you can learning about your field and your customers as possible. Remember the lessons of improvement and endurance that you learned in your passion stage. Information is vital to your growth and success.

Adding value to your brand can explode your sales expectation and shorten your learning curve for future setbacks. Yes, future setbacks. Just because you overcame the first hurdle does not mean that your business and brand won't be tested again. The more your business grows the more you need to know in order to advance to the next level.

Never be stagnant about paying for things that will add value to your life and business. You expect your customers to pay for your products, with the assurance that their lives will be enhanced from it. Invest those resources into products or that will enhance your life, and cause your brand to grow. Like this book.:) Understand the time, money and resources that you have saved because of the valuable information you have obtained. Adding valuable knowledge to your business can become one of your most invaluable sources.

BRAND BUILDING TIP:

No one knows everything, so don't come off as a know-it-all. Surround yourself with advisors and mentors who will nurture you to become a better leader and businessman. Find successful, knowledgeable individuals with whom you share common interests and mutual business goals that see value in working with you for the long-term.

BRAND BUILDING FACT:

MENTORED BUSINESSES INCREASED THEIR REVENUE BY 83% WHILE NON-MENTORED BUSINESS ONLY INCREASED THEIR REVENUE BY 16%

4. Your Dream Has Become Reality

Living your dream isn't half bad huh? For most entrepreneurs we are never satisfied with the status quo. We know and believe that there is still more that can be done and improved.

In this particular stage of developing your brand and company's growth, you should always look to achieve greater levels of success; not in just building your brand but, helping and enhancing the world. Maybe your brand does this already? If not, it may be a good way to see if it can. If you are selling apparel, maybe donate your clothing to people in need. If you are in the Tech Industry perhaps you could develop an easy to understand app, that is friendly to senior citizens who would like nothing do with technology. There are many ways that you can expand and create new avenues to your brand.

Take on new staff. Fresh faces can also bring fresh ideas that you would have never have thought of. It is better to have them on your team now than to be your competition later. Never become so attached to the business and your way of thinking that you don't lend an ear to hear what others have to say about your business. Yes, it is your business and you built it from the ground up, you are a success, but, do not neglect the people who have helped you become a success. They have validated your brand with their dollars.

While you may have reached the pinnacle of a certain part of your brand or company's growth in one area, always be on the lookout for what is new and what is possibly coming up the road. The new technology, vision or brand could be just the exact medium you need to take your brand even further.

Building your brand is no easy task. It is crowded with many obstacles and choices. Deciding what you are going to unleash to the world should be carefully thought out, prayed over and released, while doing the best you can and avoiding un-calculated risks if possible. Yes, you may fail and not get everything right when starting your brand, but just a little heads up, no one does. We all have to go through the same learning curves and stages to build up our brands. The thing that sets us apart from everyone is that we never give up on building it.

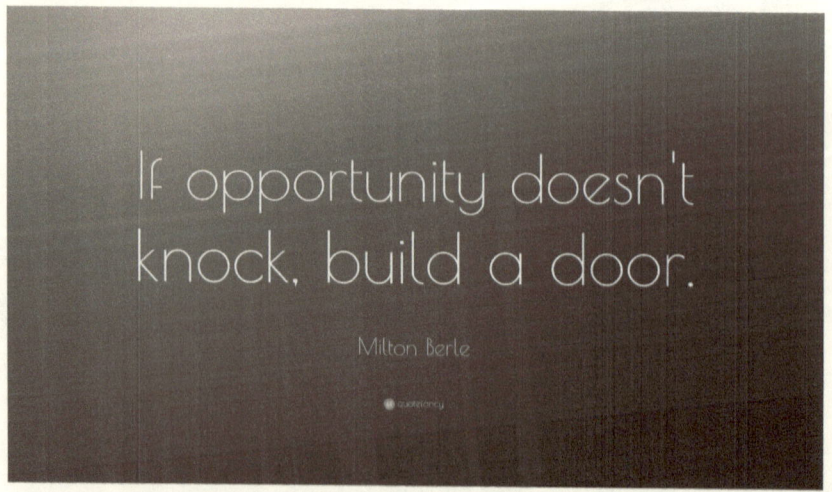

If opportunity doesn't knock, build a door.

Milton Berle

Chapter 3

Tools to get started

Channeling your ideas

You have been waiting to get your business started for as long as you could remember. Your ideas and thoughts are running rampant through your mind. Where do I start? What tools do I need to get started? How much money will I need to get started? All of these questions are going through your mind now. The best way to channel your ideas for your business is to find out as much as you can with everything that is connected to your business. As with most products, there is a plethora of information available to you to learn about your service. The internet is a great tool to find in-depth information about your product. Libraries are also an exceptional place to find out valuable information on your craft.

Know Your Niche.

Once you have decided on your product. A good rule of thumb is to find out how much it will cost to produce and reproduce it. If it is something no one has ever seen before, I would advise meeting with a patent attorney which we will highlight later in this chapter. Learn as much as you can about the product. What will make it a success and what are possible roadblocks to failure?

Educating yourself on your idea or product will be a great asset that will strengthen you in your product knowledge. This research helps to insure you don't get taken advantage of in the future. The only thing more expensive than education is ignorance.

The best way to organize ideas when starting your business, is to channel the main thought and adjoin other creative thoughts as your ideas grow. Remember to remain focused. You want a clear pathway of thinking that can guide you to the initial steps in bringing this idea to fruition. One of the greatest methods you can use to help visualize your route to success, other than writing it down in a business plan or simply with pen and paper is, a vision board. (see image below)

Vision Board from crossfitroundrocktx.com

Often, when I speak to a group of people, I encourage them to create a vision board. Why? Because we are driven by what we see. When something is in front of us consistently, we begin to gravitate towards those things or mimic them if they are behavioral.

So what is a vision board? A vision board is a tool used to help clarify, concentrate and maintain focus on a specific life goal or goals. A vision board is literally any sort of board on which you display images that represent whatever you want to be, do, or have in your life. Simply put... It's a board of your visions.

What can I use it for? It can help you to clarify and focus on your vision. Also, you can re-inforce your daily affirmations. It can also be used as a motivator and inspiration to help you fulfill your destiny both spiritually and naturally.

A vision board works well with ideas. When you have numerous ideas and goals, a vision board can help you clarify them and stay focused on achieving and maintaining them.

Put your vision board up somewhere you will see it everyday to be visually reminded of your targeted outcome.

Your ideas coupled with the visual reminder of your board is one of the first tools to get you started with your business.

Here is a list of tools you can find around the house or at an office supply store to get you started.

1. A large cardboard poster

2. Clippings from magazines and the internet

3. Scissors

4. Glue

5. A place where you can display your board so you can see it daily

6. A list of specific items you would like to see on your vision board

7. Creativity. Your vision board is a reflection of you. Let it reflect where you see yourself in the future.

Here is a link to give you a little more info on vision boards.

http://www.huffingtonpost.com/elizabeth-rider/the-scientific-reason-why_b_6392274.html

BRAND BUILDING QUOTE:

WHERE THERE IS NO VISION,
THERE IS NO HOPE.

GEORGE WASHINGTON CARVER

How much money do I need?

There is no hard and fast answer to this question. This answer can vary, with as many different businesses that there are. There are many different factors that you should consider when trying to decide how much money you may need. Here is a list taken from entrepreneur.com to help you determine how to figure out how much you may need to get started. http://www.entrepreneur.com/article/23792

MONEY, Who is going to fund this thing?

You have gotten all of your ideas down on paper. Your vision board is up and getting you motivated. You have a general idea of how much money you need to get your business started. You are ready to hit the pavement and start your million-dollar empire. There is only one problem: You do not have the funds and resources to get started.

Most of us would say, "If I had the money, why should I even start my own business?" Finding funding for your dreams is one of the most difficult tasks for most entrepreneurs.

Don't give up; there is hope. There are a variety of different methods to obtaining the funding you need. Some are more popular than others. There is also a certain resource that should be a last resort if possible.

1. Family and Friends

This is one of the first recommendations many entrepreneurs suggest because automatically you may have people close to you who would really like to support you and see you accomplish your goals. There are a lot more positives in this method than negatives. For example, many will not charge you interest and expect a huge return in the first couple of months. They may even surprise you and not only fund you but ask to be a helping hand if needed to get you started on your journey. Not saying that they won't ask for a return on their investment, but most of the time this is the best route to start.

This is sometimes called the method of **OPM** (other people's money). Start by trying to use resources other than your own, even if you have them, to fund your business. This method not only relates to money, but also connections, contacts, brands, distribution channels and whatever other resources that your friends and family may have that can help lessen the cost of starting your business. Another great resource for this is a recent book release entitled; "The Power of Broke" by Daymond John. This book gives accounts of different success stories on how entrepreneurs used many resources, their empty pockets and forged connections with people that were around them to achieve their dreams.

2. Your own money

I often say the best investment you can make is in yourself. When investing in yourself you have no one to answer to but you. If the sacrifice is big enough, you will hold yourself accountable to not making frivolous spending decisions. The cons to doing this is that if your business does not take off immediately, as you would have hoped, you can find yourself broke and disappointed. The positive is, if your business is a great hit from the jump you will not need to give up shares of your company to anyone else or repay a loan. You are the boss and sole shareholder. You call the shots and everything you say goes.

3. Crowdfunding

What is crowdfunding?

Crowdfunding is the process of raising money to fund what is typically a project or business venture through many donors using an online platform, such as Kickstarter, Indiegogo and Crowdfunder.

Using one of these platforms is a great way to get people informed of your product or business before launch. This can create (if the product is good in their eyes) word of mouth advertising, which is priceless. You can keep the funding and ask for any amount that you are seeking! The con to that is maybe no one will fund you at all. It's possible that people really would not care about your product, which could lead to you getting frustrated and not wanting to continue further.

Many new tech companies and businesses have gone this route, some to great success and some with no success at all. If you decide to go this route take some lessons from successful campaigns. Look at what may have worked for them regarding their field and product. Many of these startups offer certain incentives to the prospective funders and allow them to be on the forefront of the company's growth. It also leaves the seeders with an early connection with that product or brand.

Read books and articles about starting a successful campaign. Learn more about the brand that you want to feature to the world. Share what makes your product unique or helpful to prospective consumers. Give the world your elevator pitch on what makes you unique and special. Show them why your brand is trustworthy and valuable of their earned dollars.

One of the difficulties about this space now is that it has become crowded with people who just want free money. There are people who don't have a real plan swarming the internet to see what they can get for nothing. Set yourself apart, if you use this platform. Let the world know this is the product or business they have been waiting for and they can have an opportunity on the ground floor helping your business and brand succeed. Here are a few links to a few crowd funding websites.

Always check! Do your due diligence to find out different percentage rates, validity and policies that each of these companies offer. Do your homework upfront so you won't have to pay for it later on in your business.

https://www.kickstarter.com

https://www.indiegogo.com

https://www.gofundme.com

https://crowdfunded.com

4. Angel Investors

What are angel investors?

An angel investor or angel (also known as a business angel, informal investor, angel funder, private investor, or seed investor) is an affluent individual who provides capital for a business start-up, usually in exchange for convertible debt or ownership equity.

For many, an angel investor may be the way to go, but that decision should not be made without careful consideration. Having the right investor could catapult your company from an unknown identity to a worldwide brand in no time. The contacts and resources they have are abundant. Another plus to having an angel investor is that if they do decide to choose your company to invest in, it really says a lot about your brand as they are pitched with brands daily. For an investor to see something in your brand says a few things:

- Someone other than yourself sees the value of your brand.

- Your brand has potential to grow.

- They would like to partner with you because of your energy or work ethic.

- Your brand or product could possibly be worth millions!

With that being said, it almost seems to be a no-brainer. "Why not go with someone or a group of people that can take my idea to the next level?" What many people fail to realize is that this type of investment in you and in your company will cost. People are now more familiar with this type of investing because of the extremely popular show "Shark Tank". Countless people would love to connect with savvy business owners as those on the show do. You must not forget that they are investors and they would like an ROI (Return on Investment). For more info on ROI click here: http://www.investopedia.com/terms/r/returnon-investment.asp

Simply put, they are not going to give you something for nothing. More likely than not, the investor would like an equity stake in your company. Many investors would like you to pay back their money with 3X-5X the amount invested. Sharks they may be but, you also must calculate the value they can bring to your company or brand. Choosing an investor should be done carefully and wisely. Most of this selection is greatly dependent upon if the investor would want to invest in your product.

Preparing your pitch to an investor will be your make or break point to secure them as a partner. Search the web diligently for successful elevator pitches and what you need to do to attract the right investor.

Here is a Forbes article about 20 Things All Entrepreneurs Should Know About Angel Investors. http://www.forbes.com/sites/allbusiness/2015/02/05/20-things-all-entrepreneurs-should-know-about-angel-investors/#2715e4857a0b77a13fc6483a

5.Banks/Loans

Many startups, including myself, would like avoid this route, if possible. Starting with this type of funding already puts you in a negative cash flow, plus interest, meaning you are already in the red. On top of that, the bank can foreclose on whatever collateral attached to the loan, possibly even your business, if you fail to repay loan. My advice is if it is at all possible to avoid this risk at all costs.

For some businesses it may be a necessary evil that may need to be done if it is a retail outlet, restaurant or a larger-than-normal cost where funds cannot be obtained through another source.

The only time this route would be suggested is if you would otherwise go into debt because of inventory receivables.

Receivables are: An asset designation applicable to all debts, unsettled transactions or other monetary obligations owed to a company by its debtors or customers.

Breaking down receivables

Receivables are recorded as an asset by the company because it expects to receive payment for the outstanding amounts soon.

Read more: Receivables Definition | Investopedia http://www.investopedia.com/terms/r/receivables.asp#ixzz40UJO9ELn

In this situation, you have more orders and demand than you have money to produce the product. Even at this juncture the suggestion would be to seek other means of funding such as family or friends or one of the methods mentioned above before considering a bank loan.

Funding is one of the biggest life sources of your business. The "who" and the "how" behind the funding can make or break your business. A wise entrepreneur should always investigate which method would work best for their company and continue only when proper time, research and examination has been done.

BUSINESS STATISTIC

In a recent infographic from Bolt Insurance, one in three small business owners borrow money from family and friends, while fully 75 percent of young firms' funds come from bank loans and credit, with an average of $80,000 annual owner investment in young firms. For every $6.27 of venture capital invested since 1970, $6.27 of revenue was generated. Not everyone takes the funding route, however, as one in ten startups don't use capital injections of any sort.

Legalese

Let's say you decide to open "Nicky's Lemonade Stand" to show your children the value of hard work and a hard earned dollar. Clearly, you will not need to go deep on the legal side to get your business started. However, if you want to build a legit legal business, there are a few things you should do to get started.

I am not a lawyer, so for specific legal questions you should ask and seek a lawyer that practices law in your state as laws, and the interpretation of those laws, vary from state to state. Seek out an attorney who is well-versed in the legalities of business, and start-ups, to give you the best advice.

What should I do first?

Some of the most common questions asked by entrepreneurs include: What should I get done first, legally? Should I apply for my business license? Should I get my logo trademarked? Should I get my ideas patented? Should I incorporate my business before I do anything? These are all great questions, but sometimes a bit premature.

Prove It.

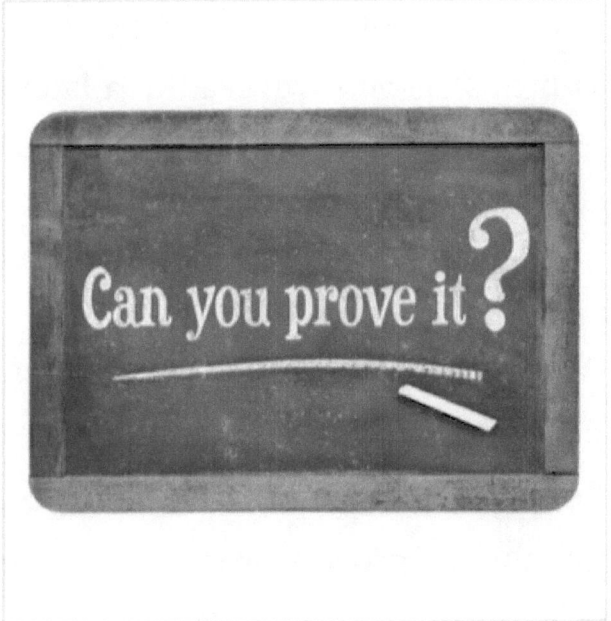

My best advice to many entrepreneurs is to first build and prove your concept. I know new entrepreneurs sometimes fear the thought of someone taking and cashing in on their valuable idea. Truth be told, most people these days are too lazy to go through the full process of stealing someones ideas and seeing it through, from conception to delivery.

In proving your concept, you must see how your product will survive in the marketplace. Is there a similar product or idea already existing in the marketplace? Is the name or logo already in use or something similar? I have personal experience with this, as you will read in a later chapter, make sure you do your research and due diligence before investing your money into the legalities of your business.

With many brands seeking a trademark, before the USPTO registers your mark, it requires that the trademark already be used in commerce or proof must be provided showing your intent to use the mark in commerce. If you apply with an "intent to use" option, you must later provide proof showing that the mark has been used within a certain amount of time after the trademark application was submitted and additional paperwork must also be submitted once the mark has been used. So before you jump into the deep end head first and pay significant amounts of money in fees, take baby steps (be diligent and move with caution and purpose) in the legal process and getting your brand started. Do what you should legally but make sure your have a market for your product before going too deep.

After you've done your due diligence and have decided that your idea or product and logo can survive in commerce, you may be ready to dive further into the legal steps in the process. At this point, it may be beneficial for you to obtain legal counsel to prepare and submit your business's formation, trademark, patent and copyright applications if applicable.

So, what is a trademark and what does it do? I often hear people use trademark, patent and copyright synonymously, but all three are totally different and protect different aspects of intellectual property. Here is a breakdown of the three:

Trademark

All information is taken from www.uspto.-gov. You may click the link for additional information. There will also be a video link at the end of this section explaining this information further. Here are the basics.

What is a trademark or service mark?

• A trademark is generally a word, phrase, symbol, or design, or a combination thereof, that identifies and distinguishes the source of the goods of one party from those of others.

• A service mark is the same as a trademark, except that it identifies and distinguishes the source of a service rather than goods. Throughout this booklet, the terms "trademark" and "mark" refer to both trademarks and service marks.

Do trademarks, copyrights, and patents protect the same things?

• No. Trademarks, copyrights, and patents protect different types of intellectual property. A trademark typically protects brand names and logos used on goods and services. A copyright protects an original artistic or literary work. A patent protects an invention. For example, if you invent a new kind of vacuum cleaner, you would apply for a patent to protect the invention itself. You would apply to register a trademark to protect the brand name of the vacuum cleaner. And you might register a copyright for the TV commercial that you use to market the product.

CONSIDERATIONS FOR FEDERAL REGISTRATION WHEN SELECTING A MARK

Once you determine that a trademark is in fact the type of protection you need is, selecting a mark is the very first step in the overall application/registration process. This must be done with thought and care, because not every mark is registrable with the USPTO nor is every mark legally protectable. That is, some marks may not be capable of serving as the basis for a legal claim by the owner seeking to stop others from using a similar mark on related goods or services. Businesses and individuals new to trademarks and the application/registration process often choose a mark for their product or service that may be difficult or even impossible to register and/or protect for various reasons. Before filing a trademark/service mark application, you should consider (1) whether the mark you want to register is registrable, and (2) how difficult it will be to protect your mark based on the strength of the mark selected. Note, the USPTO only registers marks. You, as the mark owner, are solely responsible for enforcement.

To learn more about basic trademark facts click the link to be taken to the USPTO website to download the pdf file http://www.uspto.gov/sites/default/files/BasicFacts.pdf

Video: https://www.youtube.com/watch?v=qH-DRV2NTSEk

BRAND BUILDING FACT:

IN THE "AMAZON" LOGO THE ARROW IS MORE THAN A DECORATIVE SWOOSH. THE "AMAZON" LOGO WAS CREATED TO REPRESENT THE MESSAGE THAT IT SELLS EVERYTHING FROM A TO Z. IT ALSO REPRESENTS THE SMILE CUSTOMERS WOULD EXPERIENCE FROM SHOPPING AT "AMAZON".

Copyright

What Is a Copyright?

Copyright is a form of protection provided by the laws of the United States (title 17, U.S. Code) to the authors of "original works of authorship," including literary, dramatic, musical, artistic, and certain other intellectual works. This protection is available to both published and unpublished works. Section 106 of the 1976 Copyright Act generally gives the owner of copyright the exclusive right to do and to authorize others to do the following:

- reproduce the work in copies or phonorecords

- prepare derivative works based upon the work

- distribute copies or phonorecords of the work to the public by sale or other transfer of ownership, or by rental, lease, or lending

- perform the work publicly, in the case of literary, musical, dramatic, and choreographic works, pantomimes, and motion pictures and other audio visual works

- display the work publicly, in the case of literary, musical, dramatic, and choreographic works, pantomimes, and pictorial, graphic, or sculptural works, including the individual images of a motion picture or other audiovisual work

- perform the work publicly (in the case of sound recordings*) by means of a digital audio transmission

In addition, certain authors of works of visual art have the rights of attribution and integrity as described in section 106A of the 1976 Copyright Act. For further information, see Circular 40, Copyright Registration for Works of the Visual Arts.

It is illegal for anyone to violate any of the rights provided by the copyright

law to the owner of copyright. These rights, however, are not unlimited in scope. Sections 107 through 122 of the 1976 Copyright Act establish limitations on these rights. In some cases, these limitations are specified exemptions from copyright liability. One major limitation is the doctrine of "fair use," which is given a statutory basis in section 107 of the 1976 Copyright Act. In other instances, the limitation takes the form of a "compulsory license" under which certain limited uses of copyrighted works are permitted upon payment of specified royalties and compliance with statutory conditions. For further information about the limitations of any of these rights, consult the copyright law or write to the Copyright Office.

• For more copyright information check out: http://www.copyright.gov

For the rest of the above information on copyrights click here: http://www.copyright.gov/circs/circ01.pdf

---

BRAND BUILDING FACT:

COPYRIGHT

DID YOU KNOW THAT WHENEVER YOU WRITE A POEM OR STORY OR EVEN A PAPER FOR YOUR CLASS, OR A DRAWING OR OTHER ARTWORK, YOU AUTOMATICALLY OWN THE COPYRIGHT TO IT.

Patent

What is a Patent?

A patent for an invention is the grant of a property right to the inventor, issued by the United States Patent and Trademark Office(USPTO). Generally, the term of a new patent is 20 years from the date on which the application for the patent was filed in the United States or, in special cases, from the date an earlier related application was filed, subject to the payment of maintenance fees. U.S. patent grants are effective only within the United States, U.S. territories, and U.S. possessions. Under certain circumstances, patent term extensions or adjustments may be available.

The right conferred by the patent grant is, in the language of the statute and of the grant itself, "the right to exclude others from making, using, offering for sale, or selling" the invention in the United States or "importing" the invention into the United States. What is granted is not the right to make, use, offer for sale, sell or import, but the right to exclude others from making, using, offering for sale, selling or importing the invention. Once a patent is issued, the patentee must enforce the patent without aid of the USPTO.

There are three types of patents:

1) Utility patents may be granted to anyone who invents or discovers any new and useful process, machine, article of manufacture, or composition of matter, or any new and useful improvement thereof;

2) Design patents may be granted to anyone who invents a new, original, and ornamental design for an article of manufacture; and

1) Plant patents may be granted to anyone who invents or discovers and asexually reproduces any distinct and new variety of plant.

What Can Be Patented

The United States patent law specifies the general field of subject matter that can be patented and the conditions under which a patent may be obtained.

In the language of the statute, any person who "invents or discovers any new and useful process, machine, manufacture, or composition of matter, or any new and useful improvement thereof, may obtain a patent," subject to the conditions and requirements of the law. The word "process" is defined by law as a process, act, or method, and primarily includes industrial or technical processes. The term "machine" used in the statute needs no explanation. The term "manufacture" refers to articles that are made, and includes all manufactured articles. The term "composition of matter" relates to chemical compositions and may include mixtures of ingredients as well as new chemical compounds. These classes of subject matter taken together include practically everything that is made by man and the processes for making the products.

The Atomic Energy Act of 1954 excludes the patenting of inventions useful solely in the utilization of special nuclear material or atomic energy in an atomic weapon. See 42 U.S.C. 2181(a).

The patent law specifies that the subject matter must be "useful." The term "useful" in this connection refers to the condition that the subject matter has a useful purpose and also includes operativeness, that is, a machine which will not operate to perform the intended purpose would not be called useful, and therefore would not be granted a patent.

Interpretations of the statute by the courts have defined the limits of the field of subject matter that can be patented, thus it has been held that the laws of nature, physical phenomena, and abstract ideas are not patentable subject matter.

A patent cannot be obtained upon a mere idea or suggestion. The patent is granted upon the new machine, manufacture, etc., as has been said, and not upon the idea or suggestion of the new machine. A complete description of the actual machine or other subject matter for which a patent is sought is required.

To learn more about basic patent facts click the link to be taken to the USPTO website: http://www.uspto.gov/patents

To learn more about the above information click this link: http://www.uspto.gov/patents-getting-started/general-information-concerning-patents

Poor Man's Patent and Copyright

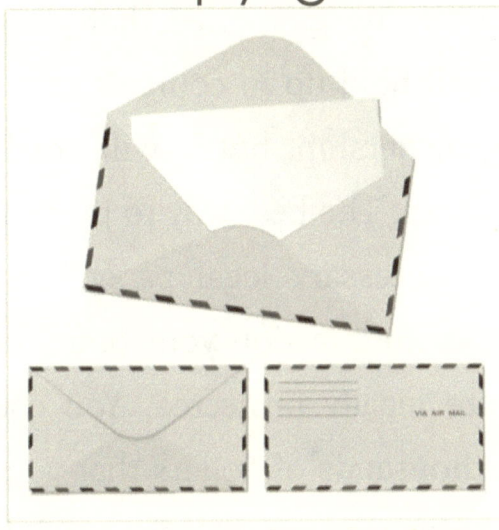

We have all heard of the saying, or heard someone else say if you want to get that patented, put it in an envelope and mail it to yourself and don't open it when you get it back. Even more secure remedies have now been added to this act of protecting your product or idea. From going to the local currency exchange or to a notary public and have them sign off on seeing this idea first. Heck, I have even tried it when starting one of my brands and musical compositions.

While this may seem like the easiest and cheapest way to protect your brand or body of work, there is no guarantee that your unopened envelope will hold up in court. It may help in determining ownership, but it will not help you to prove damages. The best way to protect yourself is to file the necessary legal paper work ensuring that there is no question your brand and/or body of work are legally protected. You could end up spending thousands of dollars that you don't have trying to prove that you had the mark first instead of paying the small fee upfront to make sure your work is protected. As always, check with an attorney who practices law in your state to find out the governing laws in protecting your product and work. Here are a few articles explaining what and what not to do to protect your work.

- http://www.avvo.com/legal-guides/ugc/is-there-a-poor-mans-trademark-like-the-poor-mans-copyright

- https://www.youtube.com/watch?v=eTLm-c99c9k4&app=desktop

- For music: https://www.youtube.com/watch?v=ehqIn2i0zHU

- https://en.wikipedia.org/wiki/Poor_man%27s_copyright

BRAND BUILDING FACT:

THE GUINNESS BOOK OF WORLD RECORDS CREDITS SHUNPEI YAMAZAKI OF JAPAN WITH HAVING THE MOST PATENTS: 6,314 IN 12 COUNTRIES AS OF 2011.

BRAND BUILDING FACT:

IN 1849, ATTORNEY ABRAHAM LINCOLN WAS GRANTED PATENT NO. 6,469 FOR A DEVICE THAT COULD BE FILLED WITH AIR TO ALLOW A SHIP TO PASS THROUGH SHOALS OR SHALLOW WATER.

HE IS THE ONLY U.S. PRESIDENT TO HOLD A PATENT

Profit Vs. Prophet

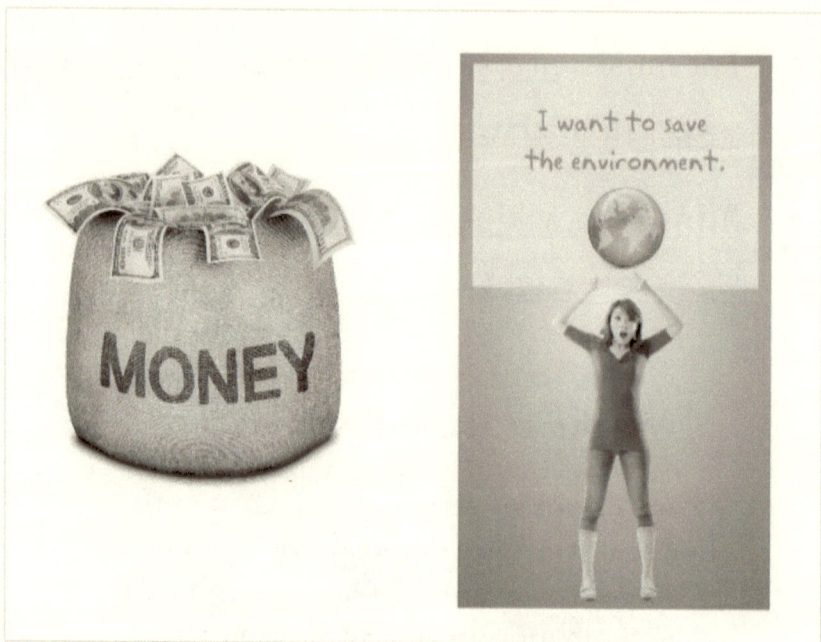

Now would be a good time to determine what kind of business you would like to form. Do you want to have a for-profit business, where you sell products and reap the financial returns, or do you want what I call a "prophet" business, where there is a certain humanitarian or environmental call or message you would like to establish for your business?

If you want to start a for-profit business, one of the first things you need to do is register your small business. A for-profit business is a business or organization whose primary goal is making money and profit.

After you determine if you want a for-profit or "prophet" business, you must also decide the type of business you are forming. There are many types of businesses you can start. Here is a list and a brief description of the more popular business startups.

• **Sole Proprietorship-** A business that legally has no separate existence from its owner. Income and losses are taxed on the individual's personal income tax return.

The sole proprietorship is the simplest business form under which one can operate a business. The sole proprietorship is not a legal entity. It simply refers to a person who owns the business and is personally responsible for its debts. A sole proprietorship can operate under the name of its owner or it can do business under a fictitious name, such as Nancy's Nail Salon. The fictitious name is simply a trade name--it does not create a legal entity separate from the sole proprietor owner. For more info: http://www.entrepreneur.com/encyclopedia/sole-proprietorship

Partnership- A legal form of business operation between two or more individuals who share management and profits. The federal government recognizes several types of partnerships. The two most common are general and limited partnerships.

If your business will be owned and operated by several individuals, you'll want to take a look at structuring your business as a partnership. Partnerships come in two varieties: general partnerships and limited partnerships. In a general partnership, the partners manage the company and assume responsibility for the partnership's debts and other obligations. A limited partnership has both general and limited partners. The general partners own and operate the business and assume liability for the partnership, while the limited partners serve as investors only; they have no control over the company and are not subject to the same liabilities as the general partners. For more info: http://www.entrepreneur.com/encyclopedia/partnership

Corporation- A form of business operation that declares the business as a separate, legal entity guided by a group of officers known as the board of directors.

A corporate structure is perhaps the most advantageous way to start a business because the corporation exists as a separate entity. In general, a corporation has all the legal rights of an individual, except for the right to vote and certain other limitations. Corporations are given the right to exist by the state that issues their charter. If you incorporate in one state to take advantage of liberal corporate laws but do business in another state, you'll have to file for "qualification" in the state in which you wish to operate the business. There's usually a fee that must be paid to qualify to do business in a state. For more information: http://www.entrepreneur.com/encyclopedia/corporation

Limited Liability Company (LLC)- A Limited Liability Company (LLC) is a business structure allowed by state statute. Each state may use different regulations, and you should check with your state if you are interested in starting a Limited Liability Company. This business structure combines the pass-through taxation of a partnership or sole proprietorship with the limited liabilities of a corporation.

Owners of an LLC are called members. Most states do not restrict ownership, and so members may include individuals, corporations, other LLCs and foreign entities. There is no maximum number of members. Most states also permit "single-member" LLCs, those having only one owner.

For more information: https://www.irs.gov/Businesses/Small-Businesses-&-Self-Employed/Limited-Liability-Company-LLC

Nonprofit Organization- A business organization that serves some public purpose and therefore enjoys special treatment under the law. Nonprofit corporations, contrary to their name, can make a profit but can't be designed primarily for profit-making.

When it comes to your business structure, have you thought about organizing your venture as a nonprofit corporation? Unlike a for-profit business, a nonprofit may be eligible for certain benefits, such as sales, property and income tax exemptions at the state level. The IRS points out that while most federal tax-exempt organizations are nonprofit organizations, organizing as a nonprofit at the state level doesn't automatically grant you an exemption from federal income tax.

For more information:http://www.entrepreneur.com/encyclopedia/nonprofit-corporation

Here are a few helpful links to help you get started when trying to decide what type of business you want to create. They are filled with valuable information. Take your time as you search through the information to find out what is right for you.

- Small Business General info: https://www.sba.gov

- Register your business in your state: https://www.sba.gov/content/register-with-state-agencies

- How to start a 501C3: https://www.501c3.org/how-to-start-a-501c3-nonprofit/

- IRS 501C3 information I: https://www.irs.gov/Charities-&-Non-Profits/Application-for-Recognition-of-Exemption

- IRS 501C3 information II: https://www.irs.gov/Charities-&-Non-Profits/Charitable-Organizations

What is your "Why?"

In the middle of gathering all the tools that you will need to get your business started, you need to ask yourself "Why?"

The reason I put this in the middle of the tools section is because in the middle of getting your business started and being introduced to the beginning of many failures on your journey to success, you will come to a point when you will ask yourself "why?" Why am I doing this? Why am I wasting all my time, energy and resources for this idea? Why am I consistently trying to bring this idea or business to fruition and all I get are no's and rejection.

When you get to this point, your "Why?" has to be strong enough to sustain you through all of your rejections. Your "Why?" has to be engrained deep enough into your being that regardless of what opposition you are faced with, or how large the task ahead may be, or the difficulties you are facing now in the infancy of your business, your why has to be, BIGGER, STRONGER, and more PRONOUNCED in your life than everything that your are currently enduring.

Maybe it is for your children to have a better life? You may want a better home than what you have now, Maybe you want to change the world with your idea and help the homeless. Regardless of what your motive may be, your "Why?" will be the guiding force to sustain you in your lowest moments.

When you are at these moments, it would be a good time to take a look at your vision board and remember the passion that got you started. The reason you are creating this brand or business is greater than the opposition you may be facing. So, when those difficult times arise look at your vision board or within yourself and see the final result;.Then tell yourself "That's Why!"

BRAND BUILDING QUOTE:

THERE ARE TWO GREAT DAYS IN A PERSON'S LIFE - THE DAY WE ARE BORN AND THE DAY WE DISCOVER WHY.

WILLIAM BARCLAY

The Designer

Unless you have been given the ability to be the creative genius behind your brand and have the God given talent to draw, like many you will need to hire a designer. Sometimes this can be overlooked but it is very important in creating your brand or products.

Your relationship with the designer has great significance. You need to be able to relate what you see in your mind's eye into a 2D or 3D representation of what you want. It is from there that the designer will have to transfer your thoughts into a vivid image for your manufacturer to produce. If you have a product other than T-shirts or printed items, you may need to have a designer that can make a tech pack.

What is a tech pack?

A tech pack is an informative sheet which encompasses all the specifications of the requirements before embarking on the manufacturing process. It contains all the details of any specific style of the product. This document is usually prepared by the designer and finalized in consultation with the merchandisers, and then forwarded to bulk sampling department or to the production department for the reference and guide for bulk manufacturing.

Why do you need a tech pack?

With a tech pack, designers and companies are more likely to get a sample or product made correctly with minimal errors. Supplying a tech pack to a manufacturer gives them a concrete guideline to your product, so without one it can be difficult for manufacturers to translate your idea into an actual product. It also allows the manufacturer to make a product without having to refer back to the designer several times. When creating products, manufacturers can reference the tech pack to make sure they aren't overlooking any aspect of your design.

(Sample of what a tech packs may look like)

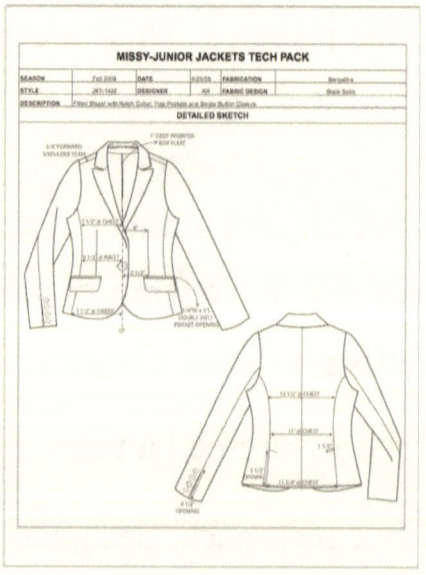

Here is where good word of mouth can come in handy. If you know of someone or have heard of someone who can draw, now would be a good time to give that budding artist a shot.

There are also a number of websites that you can search and find designers for various prices for numerous products and projects. As with anything being suggested from anyone, always do your homework before locking in an agreement with anyone. Here is a resource and website that I have found to be helpful in garnering small design services and for an additional fee you can utilize other services that the designer may offer. https://www.fiverr.com

---

BRAND BUILDING TIP:

FOR FINDING THE RIGHT DESIGNER

Make sure that you're both clear about revisions. Many designers include a set number of revisions in their project packages. Make sure that you understand what constitutes a revision, how many you'll get and what happens once they're all used up.

Manufacturing

Who's going to produce my idea?

So, you have a great product and have sourced sufficient funding to start your idea. All of your legal work is done, but you don't know where or how to get it manufactured.

Google searches and online research can only take you so far. You have so many responses or recommendations from your searches but you have no idea if they would be a perfect fit for your company. You seem to have more questions about your search results than answers to your original question. Can I trust this company? Will they steal my idea? How long have they been around? What is their reputation in the industry? These are some of the many questions that you are faced with when trying to secure manufacturing or a supplier for your product.

Truth be told, there is no guaranteed answer to this question. This is where your homework and research is critical. Can you research a company to the best of your ability and it still not be a great relationship? Yes. Unfortunately, even some of the best companies you discover through a word of mouth recommendation can have you pulling out your hair. One method that has worked for me is narrowing down to 2 to 3 companies that I am considering and giving them all a shot. I send out a small sample order and see who responds and produces my product as close to my liking as possible. Here is a checklist that I have when I am looking to use a new manufacturer.

1. How long have they been in business?

2. Is there a language barrier?

3. Do they specialize in this product?

4. Are they working with larger brands who sell similar products?

5. How quickly are they in responding to me?

6. How low are their minimums?

7. How much is shipping from the place of origin?

8. Where are they securing and sourcing the materials to produce my product from?

9. Are their factories up to code with labor laws?

10. What are the reviews on this company?

11. Are they unnecessarily anxious about getting my business?

12. How long will it take to produce and deliver my product in mass quantities?

13. Will they sign a nondisclosure agreement?

14. Will they offer my money back if they don't deliver on time?

15. What is my gut saying?

Though this is a long checklist to implement, I have found it has saved me much time and headaches doing all the research upfront. When you have the perfect manufacture or producer of your goods it is like the perfect marriage with a partner who is just as concerned about delivering you quality products and services, as you are about selling them to your consumers.

Creating a strong relationship with your manufacturer can have so many great benefits to the budding business. Why? Because just as you are looking for a reliable company to produce your goods. They are looking for a company to do well in sales and build a great relationship. So, as your company grows, you will continue to patronize them as your manufacturer and this keeps their business strong as well.

U.S or Overseas?

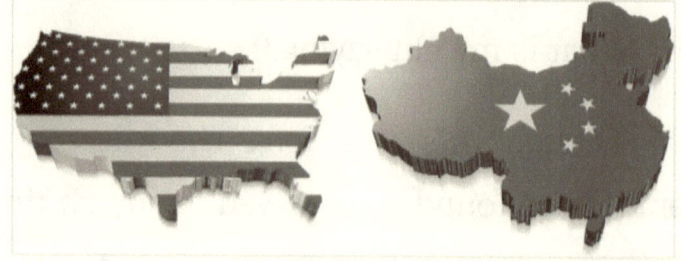

Are you feeling patriotic? This is a difficult question for some and a no-brainer for others. Where should I get my goods manufactured?

Many would like to keep as many jobs as possible in the good old USA and build the economy of our nation before building another. There is a feeling of patriotism knowing that you helped your country, state or local counties economy by producing your products stateside. Many find it difficult to achieve any profit because the margins are so low and its difficult to grow a profitable company.

Other businesses may have the sentiment of, once I get my company off the ground I will have certain initiatives and capital to build up my company stateside. Regardless of what side of the fence you find yourself on, there are still many pros and cons that must be compared on both sides before making a decision.

This can be a difficult choice with some business owners. Being left with a feeling as if you are letting your country down, or you have failed to participate in your fellow American duty to not leave your brother behind. On the other hand, you are struggling to make a profit and if you can't make a profit you can't help anyone.

Here are a few pros and cons to help you weed through the decision-making process.

PROS: (Manufacturing in the USA)

- You are able to help your local economy grow.

- Ability to keep a closer eye on your products and the manufacturing process.

- Have the inward gratification that your products are made in the USA

- Little to no language barriers.

- Low shipping and export tax costs.

- Tax deductions for manufacturing stateside.

- State laws to protect your product or brand.

CONS: (Manufacturing in the USA)

- Your manufacturer is really a middleman, and is still shipping your product overseas for manufacturing. (This really happens.)

- Lower profit margins.

- Higher costs to produce goods.

- Not many factories to produce certain goods.

- Need more capital to produce the same amount of goods compared to less capital for overseas manufacturing.

PROS: (For manufacturing outside the USA)
- Lower price per unit cost.

- Higher profit margins.

- You help other causes stateside because of revenue and profits you have earned.

- There are services that can be used to help with the language barrier to insure product accuracy.

CONS: (For manufacturing outside the USA)

- You are growing another country's economy.

- You take away jobs that could possibly be done locally.

- You cannot be in or travel to that country as often as you would like to oversee and check out the process.

- Language barriers.

- High shipping and export tax cost.

- Products being held up for inspection at the customs office.

- A delay on getting your products as promised. (When bigger brands and companies place orders.)

- No laws to protect your product or brand.

- Rising cost of manufacturing.

- Child labor practices.

- High order volume to get lower pricing.

As you can see, there are many pros and cons and arguments that can be made for both cases. It is up to you to be a wise business owner and to count the costs to see what works best for your business.

Also beware of stateside businesses that claim to manufacture your products stateside. They build their business on being the middleman and actually end up shipping and manufacturing your product overseas.

Here are a few articles to help you make a decision on manufacturing:

- http://fortune.com/2015/06/26/fracking-manufacturing-costs/

- http://www.bloomberg.com/bw/articles/2014-04-25/china-vs-dot-the-u-dot-s-dot-its-just-as-cheap-to-make-goods-in-the-u-dot-s-dot-a

If you choose to manufacture overseas here are a few websites to start your search.

- Alibaba http://www.alibaba.com

- Global Sources http://www.globalsources.-com

- Made in China http://www.made-in-china.-com

As always do your due diligence and research before doing business with any company both overseas and domestic.

> **BRAND BUILDING FACT:**
>
> There are 12.33 million manufacturing workers in the United States, accounting for 9 percent of the workforce.

Website

Websites are essential for any business to grow and survive. Your website is the hub and connecting point between you and your consumer. A good website works for you 24/7 whether you are sleep or on vacation. This is necessary for all businesses.

For many who may have been caught in a time warp or rather not care to go this route I will briefly describe what a website is.

What is a website? A location connected to the Internet that maintains one or more pages on the World Wide Web.

A website, also written as web site,[1] or simply site,[2] is a set of related web pages typically served from a single web domain. A website is hosted on at least one web server, accessible by way of a network such as the Internet or a private local area network through an Internet address known as a uniform resource locator (URL). All publicly accessible websites collectively constitute the World Wide Web.

Here is a link to find out more about websites: https://en.wikipedia.org/wiki/Website

BUSINESS KEY: When you have decided on your company's or brand's name IMMEDIATELY go and acquire the domain name!

To thrive in the ever changing world of commerce you need a website to inform your customers, sell product and let the consumer know what is going on with your brand.

Your website should be an extension of your brand. It should duplicate the essence of what you are trying to sell or convey to your consumer. It should be very informative and look professional. Regardless of the area of your business, it should always look professional.

The importance of having a professional looking website says a lot about you and your brand. Your website is a reflection of you. It is a window where customers can search and find out all the necessary information that they need to know about your company. Your presentation is key! Many people lose sales just by how their website looks alone. You would not want to shop at a rundown store for quality products and neither will your consumers. Give your customers an experience like none other. Here are some helpful do's and don'ts when creating your website.

DO:

- Make sure your website is professional.

- Make sure all the necessary contact information is located on your site.

- Make sure your mission statement is clear. (Do you want the consumer to buy, trade, sell or support your product or brand?)

- Make sure your color and theme matches the tone of your business. (If you have a luxury line of watches you should not have a Sponge Bob picture in the background.)

- If necessary, pay a professional to create a website for you. (In most cases you get what you pay for, so cheaper is not always better.)

- Make the titles on your webpage make sense. Focus on what's important. (Inform the consumer.)

- Make sure your site can be viewed on a mobile device or tablet.

- Use a reputable merchant if you are selling products, such as PayPal, Visa, MasterCard, American Express.

- Keep your website up to date.

- Have a signup sheet for consumers to signup if they choose to stay in contact with your brand. This is a good customer retention strategy.

- Make sure your site is easy to navigate.

- Make sure you have links to your social media sites.

DON'T:

- Skimp out on paying for a great website (Hey this is your business! BUT don't overpay. Find a happy medium.)

- Forget your contact information.

- Overload your page with unnecessary pictures.

- Have music in the background. (If you do choose to have music make sure that it is not loud and distracting.)

- Have flashing and twirling text all over the place. (Unless you work for the circus, leave this alone.)

- Have under construction pages. If the page is not ready, don't make it live.

- Waste your time on long flash intros (You only have a few seconds to keep the consumer's interest.)

- Create unnecessary automatic popup windows. (Consumers really hate those!) *Unless you are trying to get them to sign up for your site.

- Try not to redirect visitors off your website. You may lead them to another site and they can totally forget about you.

- Use busy backgrounds. Keep it simple.

- Be careful using all caps in certain areas, it can come off as you yelling at your consumer.

- Don't place irrelevant ads across your page.

- Don't make your reader search to find something.

- Don't have dead links.

As you can see having a webpage can become a little complicated. Don't worry about getting everything right, find out what works for you and your brand. Over time your website will change as you and your brand evolves. Make sure you listen to your consumers if you are hearing a constant suggestion about something. Look into getting a solution to it quickly.

Many customers shopping experiences are happening online. The growth for online sales is projected to increase see: http://www.statista.com/topics/871/online-shopping/

Although there is still a desire for many consumers to have the brick and mortar shopping experience, upon interaction with a retail store many consumers rely on online shopping to buy products once they have grown accustom to that company's sizing and product offerings.

Your website is the consumers one-stop shop and your opportunity to gain a customer and word of mouth advertising for life or lose a would-be customer in a matter of seconds. It is imperative that you take the creation and upkeep of your website serious and make sure your consumer has a pleasant shopping experience.

Here is a list of well-known domain site providers that you can check out and purchase your domain name. **Also as with anything, always compare and do your personal research to see what is the best fit for your brand.**

1.   Network Solutions http://www.networksolutions.com

2.   GoDaddy https://www.godaddy.com

3.   Wix https://www.wix.com

BRAND BUILDING FACT:

- Nearly All Consumers (97%) Now Use Online Media to Shop Locally.

- 93% Of Business Purchase Decisions Start With A Search Engine Search.

An App for your brand?

Along with your website you might also want to consider getting an application (app) created. This is a quick icon that a consumer can download on their phone and/or tablet enabling them to stay connected with your company or brand.

Just like the website, your app should be an extension of your brand. To keep your app interesting, it is a good rule of thumb to have some content that can only be app accessible by way of your app. This will keep your customers involved in finding out information about your company and brand through various means of media communication.

Some companies' apps mirror their website for the customer who rarely uses a desktop computer. Once you have a good feel for your customer base, see which medium drives the most traffic to your business by way of website or your app. You can then began optimizing that platform in greater detail to suit your customers' needs.

BRAND BUILDING FACT:

- THERE ARE 224 MILLION MONTHLY ACTIVE APP USERS IN THE US. (2014)

- DURING THE LAST FOUR YEARS, THE PERCENTAGE OF APPS USED 11 OR MORE TIMES INCREASED TO 39% IN 2014

SEO

What is SEO?

Search engine optimization (SEO) is the process of affecting the visibility of a website or a web page in a search engine's unpaid results - often referred to as "natural," "organic," or "earned" results. For more information http://searchengineland.com/guide/what-is-seo

Why is SEO so important?

An important aspect of SEO is making your website easy for both users and search engine robots to understand. Although search engines have become increasingly sophisticated, they still can't see and understand a web page the same way a human can. SEO helps the engines figure out what each page is about, and how it may be useful for users.

Many businesses are successful or fail because of great or poor SEO. The SEO lets consumers find you and the various search engines know that you are out there on the web. This can be very confusing for the new entrepreneur who just wants to get their business off the ground and not worry about dealing with the backend of a website.

This very important process can be a great asset to your company. If your customers can find you, they can buy product. If you customers can reach your product online they can buy, share, and become great advertising for your business by sharing it in various digital forms of communication, through social media, blogs, vlogs and their own websites.

Getting traffic to your online business is like purchasing real estate in a very prominent and desirable area. SEO is something that should not be taken lightly. Many companies will try to solicit your business to create an SEO package for you. As with all things, research a company out and ask questions to other users and inquire if it added anything to their sales or increased traffic to other parts of their business.

Most do-it-yourself websites now offer simple SEO solutions. You input the information and it will then create the SEO for your website automatically. This may not be the top-of-the-line professional service you may attain by patronizing another business, but it is a starting point and will help directing traffic to your business.

Treat your website as a brick and mortar business, it is your online presence to a digital world. Making sure you have a professional built website, exceptional SEO and a great product offering can assist in growing your business' revenue in a new digital age of selling products.

Your website is a representation and a reflection of your brand and products. Make sure when someone comes into your digital house, they feel welcomed. You want your customers to search, spend and interact with your brand and website. Let them learn about you, your product offerings and your message to the world.

BRAND BUILDING TIP:

Fresh content can help improve your SEO rankings. Add new, useful content to your pages on a regular basis. Content freshness adds relevancy to your site in the eyes of the search engines.

Business Cards

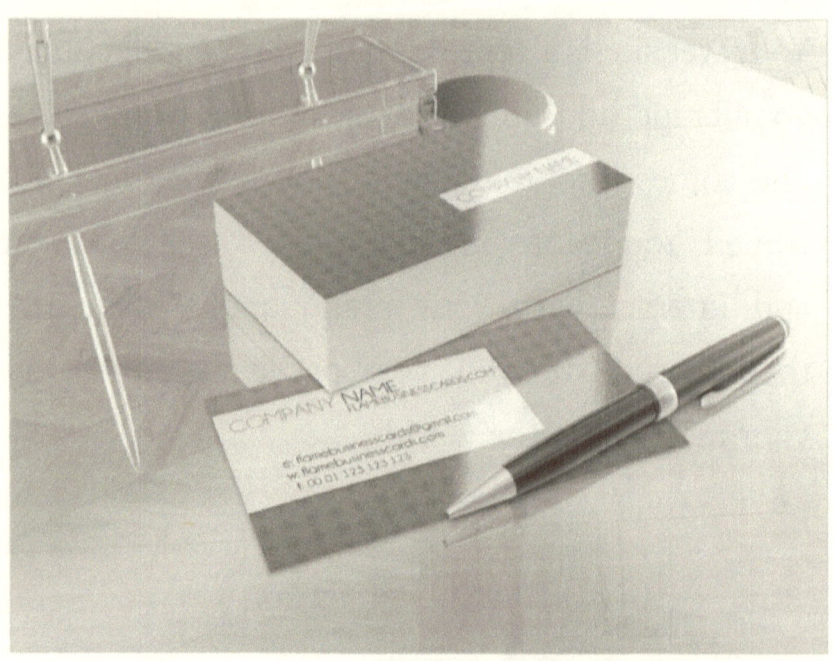

There is nothing like this old and faithful staple in the business world. That's right, the ever-present business card. Just like your website, your business card should be an extension of your product or brand. Over time, the designs and forms of business cards have changed and are ever evolving. (Remember the compact disk business cards.)

Some may say there is no right or wrong way to let your creativity run free on your business card, which in many cases may be true but, there are still some fundamental aspects that still must be adhered to. Here is a helpful chart of do's and don'ts when creating your business cards.

DO	DON'T	DO	DON'T	DO
MAKE SURE ALL OF YOUR INFORMATION IS ON THE CARD	BE OFF BRAND. YOUR CARD SHOULD BE CONSISTENT WITH YOUR COMPANIES BRAND	KEEP IT SIMPLE	USE CHEAP OR THIN PAPER	USE CUSTOM FINISHES
TRY NEW MATERIAL (OTHER THAN YOUR BASIC STOCK OF PAPER)	USE PERFORATED CARD EDGES (IF NOT ON PURPOSE)	KEEP IT STANDARD SIZE	USE COMMON CLIP ART	USE THE BACK OF THE CARD
INCLUDE YOUR WEBSITE	MAKE YOUR CLIENTS LOOK HARD TO FIND INFO.	ADD YOUR TAG LINE	USE A CHEAP PRINTER.	ALWAYS PROOFREAD YOUR CARD. ALWAYS!
INCLUDE YOUR SOCIAL MEDIA SITES	OVER CROWED YOUR CARD WITH TO MUCH TEXT	GET A PROFESSIONAL DESIGN/DESIGNER	USE MANY COLORS	USE READABLE TEXT
TRY ADDING A QR CODE TO KEEP THINGS FRESH	LET YOUR 5-YEAR OLD DESIGN YOUR CARD.	ADD YOUR LOGO FOR BRANDING PURPOSES	USE GRAINY PHOTOS	HAVE A PROFESSIONAL PRINT IT

Business card quick tip: Take your time before presenting your card. No one likes card pushers. Let the conversation grow organically. If there is an opportunity during or after your conversation, then offer your card. This is one of the best ways to be remembered as a contact.

Along with business cards, most of the information on the chart can be used with flyers or different print media used to advertise your company. I have included a link to give you some inspiration for various business card designs.

Remember, your business card may be the first extension of your brand or business that customers may see. Make sure it is a great representation of yourself, your company and your brand.

Here are a few companies to check out for design inspiration.

- The Design Inspiration http://thedesigninspiration.com/category/business-cards/

- Card Nerd http://www.cardnerd.com

- Design Inspiration http://designspiration.net/search/saves/?q=business%20card

- Hongkiat http://www.hongkiat.com/blog/minimalistic-business-card-designs/

BRAND BUILDING FACT:

NUMBER OF BUSINESS CARDS PRINTED DAILY

27,397,260

NUMBER OF BUSINESS CARDS PRINTED IN THE U.S. ANNUALLY

10,000,000,000

COMPANY SALES INCREASE FOR EVERY 2,000 CARDS PASSED OUT

2.5%

Connecting with likeminded people

Connecting with the right people is a great way to keep motivated. There is a contagious energy that is released when you are connected to people that are on the same page of success as you. You can learn from each other and encourage one another along the way. When you are down, they can lift you up and vice-versa. However, never bet all of your fortune on someone else building you up and keeping you encouraged. Use them as a tool to go higher, but not as a match to light your fire. Your passion is the spark that launched your business and sees it to fruition.

Connecting with likeminded entrepreneurs gives you a good network of contacts and information. These are people who have the same mentality that you have to make it against the odds. Networking together opens up opportunities and growth for everyone.

> ## BRAND BUILDING QUOTE:
>
> ## COMMUNICATION - THE HUMAN CONNECTION - IS THE KEY TO PERSONAL AND CAREER SUCCESS.
>
> PAUL J. MEYER

Chapter 4

Social Media

Nowadays if you don't tweet, Snapchat, Instagram, watch their live broadcast on Periscope and are not connected with people on Facebook you will get left behind this social media storm.

Parts of learning social media comes with adapting too a new lingo or social verbiage such as: OMG, SMH, LOL, BRB, BTW, POTD, and a ton of others that you being an entrepreneur must understand to clearly connect with the voice of this new generation. If you are completely oblivious to what is being said, here is a quick guide to some of the most popular internet and social media slang. http://internetslang.com

First things First

When you believe that you have the name for your business, immediately go to all the main social media avenues (Facebook, Instagram, Twitter, etc.) that you will be using to promote and inform people about your company and sign-up and create your page.

As mentioned in the legal chapter, these are some of the methods that you can utilize to begin to establish your brand even before seeking legal council.

SIDE NOTE: If you have not done this, I admonish you to go and acquire your names on social media ASAP. Your name can be taken just that fast.

Here are links to get you started to the most popular social media sites

- **Facebook** http://www.facebook.com/

- **Twitter** http://www.twitter.com/

- **Pinterest** http://www.pinterest.com/

- **Instagram** http://www.instagram.com/

- **Snapchat** https://www.snapchat.com

- **Youtube** https://www.youtube.com

- **Blogger** https://www.blogger.com

I am aware that there are plenty of other social sites but, securing these depending on your area of business should be enough to get you started.

It is very important to do this first. I often tell people when I'm talking to them in a business meeting or on the street; "Stop what you are doing right now and go and acquire your business name on social media, especially Facebook!" As of January 2016 Facebook has over 1.038 billion active daily users! You do not want the problem of someone beating you to the punch with your business name on this or any other sites. It makes it that much harder to differentiate yourself and someone else using the name. To make matters worse it could be someone who is not even using it for business purposes; it could be a teen creating a webpage just for fun. I tell many clients when you have an idea that you feel strong about or have been contemplating for a while, go and acquire the name on social media and the web domain. This step is pivotal in the foundation process of building your brand.

So many people have had to alter their business name or change certain letters in their name or company's name because it was already taken or in use by someone else. Others, have even had to start from scratch using a different name or brand because of the power of social media.

Always Something New

You as a business owner must realize that there is always something new on the horizon. Be it a new social media platform or a new way to drive customer content. Keep your ears and eyes open so you can determine what is taking off and what seems to be a quick fad.

Keeping a consistent flow of design and information will make it easier to transition to newer platforms and can instantly help your existing customers find and distinguish your content and brand.

Being consistent in social media is critical to keeping your fan base consistent. If you acquire new users through one of your media outlets and then connect them to your different online platforms and it is not consistent or updated; you will then begin to see a decline in your customer base because of not updating your platforms with your changing information. A good rule of thumb is to always keep your content fresh to keep your consumers interest.

Whatever platform you choose to build your social media on, be consistent. Whatever it is that you do, do it well. These particular social sites may be the first gateway people may stumble upon when first seeing and hearing about your brand.

Keep your content balanced in a well-organized structure to promote interest on all of your platforms. If you are selling products, you should want your social media attractive enough to direct traffic to your website or e-commerce store. Conversely, you should want your website to also drive traffic to your social media outlets where you can give consumers more content on your brand and what's to come.

All of these tools should work hand in hand as a well-oiled machine, with one platform balancing the other. Concluding with the end result of keeping your consumers happy and informed.

Dealing with social media can become a bit overwhelming. I know you are saying as the entrepreneur, "Hey I just wanna design or bake" or do whatever your major skill set may be and not deal with social media at all because, it sounds like a second job along with everything else I am doing. Truth be told, it is. Social media is not a simple task if done correctly. Many companies have started their businesses by just taking care of your social media business for you, while you take care of other parts of your business. To some business owners this may be helpful, but if you are pitching pennies and being frugal with what you have, there are many alternatives to help you run a successful social media campaign.

There are many apps and tools such as Hootsuite and others to help you update and release content on a variety of social media platforms with just one click. Search out different apps and sites and see which one works for you the best until you are able to acquire help with your social media platforms.

BRAND BUILDING FACT:

56% OF AMERICANS HAVE A PROFILE ON A SOCIAL NETWORKING SITE

Giveaways/Contests

No matter who they are, or where they are, people always love a giveaway or some type of free merchandise. You should implement this strategy when trying to gain new business and increase customer retention. Let new consumers know that you would appreciate their support, while letting your consistent customer base know that you appreciate their loyalty. Thank you goes a long way, when you implement various methods and strategies to inform your customers that you appreciate them for their loyalty and continued support.

Contests are a good way to get people involved in promoting your brand or product. You can have your consumers working for you, and pay them with a reward of your choosing. The greater the reward the greater the involvement in your customers spreading your message or brand.

Setting up a contest works for you in various ways and has more pluses than minuses. The minus is that maybe you will give away product or a huge discount. The pluses include the customer wearing your product, sharing it with the world, newly acquired customers, new revenue, new word of mouth, and with great products and services, a customer for life.

Don't Always Sale

I know that you are probably saying huh? It is my job to sell products and make a profit. Just like you, people do not want to be badgered or beaten over the head all the time about YOUR PRODUCT, YOUR SALES, YOUR COMPANY YOUR! YOUR! YOUR!

Build a relationship with your consumer. Let them grow a connection with you. Inform them that there is a caring heart behind the brand. Educate them about issues that you are concerned about in the world. Relay to them about world topics as they become relevant on social media or in your niche of business.

BRAND BUILDING FACT:

64% OF PEOPLE CITE SHARED VALUES AS THE MAIN REASON THEY HAVE A RELATIONSHIP WITH A BRAND.

Connecting with a brand

People want to connect with a brand. A feeling, of belonging to a special group or product. They want to be family. Learning this step will take you further than your greatest product. When people believe in you, your product or brand, there is nothing they won't do for you. In the business of sales you do not need fair-weather customers. Having a strong customer base can carry you through the lean times of your company and make you a strong, lasting brand.

The infographic below from <u>One Deep Design</u> gives you 6 ways to make your customers fall in love with you.

1.**Provide great customer service**. Go the extra mile to satisfy their needs because 89% of customers stop doing business with a company after experiencing poor customer service.

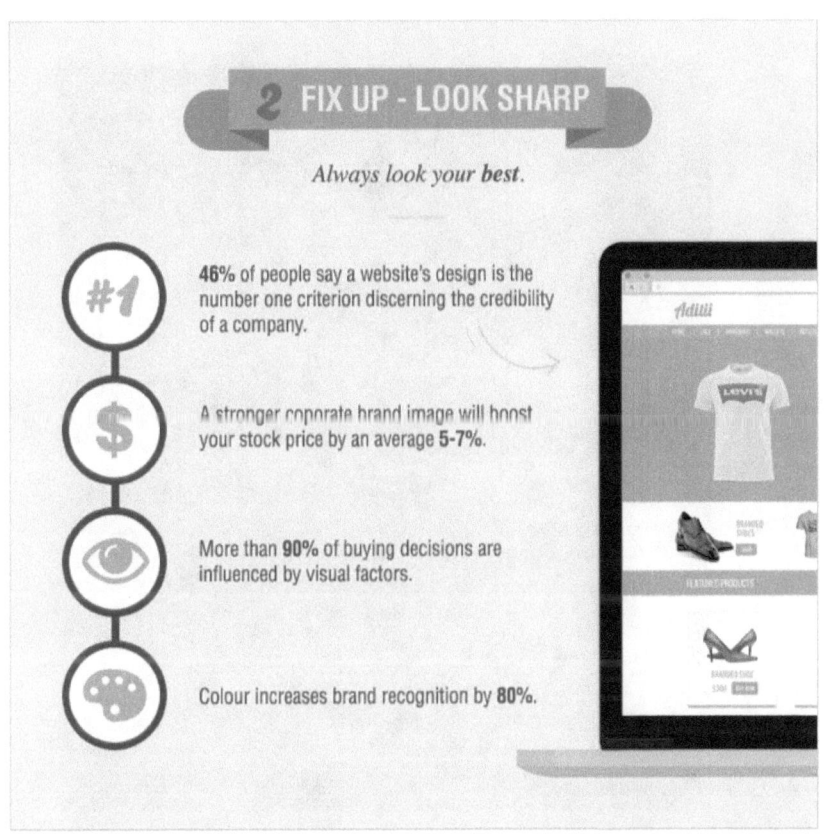

2. **Have a great brand identity.** 46% of people say a website's design is the number one criterion discerning the credibility of a company (don't cut corners here, spend the necessary resources to button-up your brand)

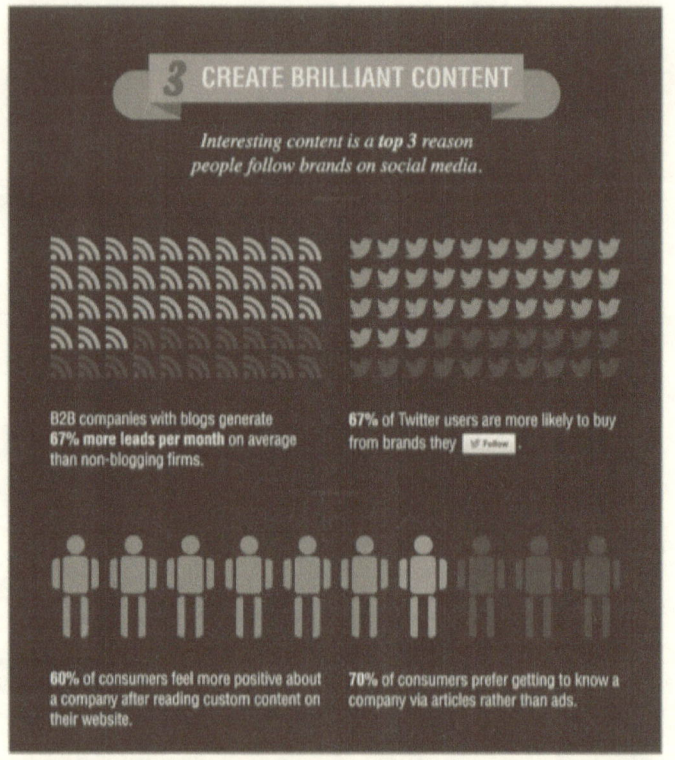

1. **Create brilliant content.** Interesting content is one of the top 3 reasons people follow brands on social media. **B2B** companies, with blogs generate more traffic than those who don't and Twitter users buy from brands they follow. **B2B(business-to-business), also known as e-biz, is the exchange of products, services or information (aka e-commerce) between businesses, rather than between businesses and consumers.**

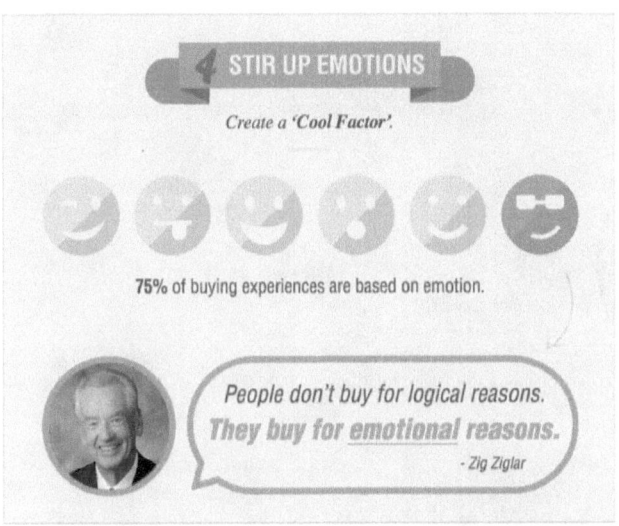

4. Create a cool factor. People don't buy for logical reasons. They buy for emotional reasons.

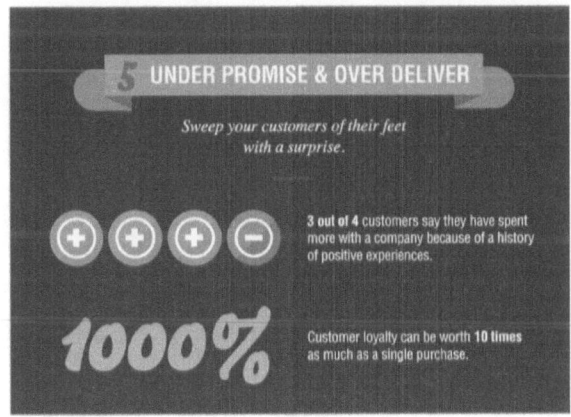

5. Under promise and over deliver.

3 out of 4 customers say they have spent more with a company because of a history of positive experiences.

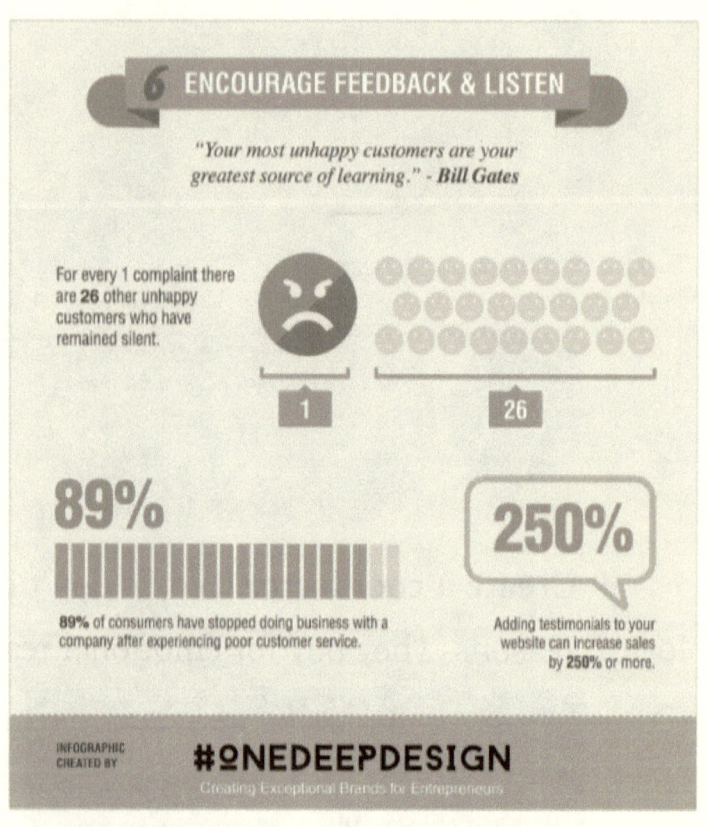

6. **Add testimonials to your website.**

Adding testimonials to your website can increase sales by 250% or more.

For more info check out One Deep Designs. http://onedeepdesign.com.au/infographic-6-ways-to-make-customers-fall-in-love-with-your-brand/

Be Prepared

Just as much as your consumers can build up your brand on social media, they can tear it down as well. The freedom of social media is that, people can be social and say whatever they want about your brand. You can block them or delete their comments from your page but you can't stop the way they feel. You cannot stop them if they choose to dislike or discredit your brand on a page of their own or on a competitor's page. Consumers can be like the wind. You are the greatest product known to man one day, and the worst of the worst the next.

With that being said, make sure that your customer service is always on point. I have seen where someone has tried to go off on a particular brand and before the brand has a chance to respond, some of the brand's consumers are already standing in the brand's defense. This should not be a method that you depend on to ward off the attacks of your brand. This is your brand. You should be the first line of defense and be able to give an appropriate response to that customer's concern or complaint.

Just as much as a bad complaint can turn a watchful eye on you, so can the praise of a loyal customer. All it takes is the right customer or celebrity, in many cases, to like or talk about your brand. Before you know it, you are on a totally new platform of exposure. As you begin to experience the complexities of social media be prepared to deal with the bad as well as the good.

Listen

Maybe that loud mouth customer's or complaint really did have a valid point. After being burned so many other times with other brands, they decided to let you have it. Either way, if they have spent their hard earned money on your product or services, they deserve your listening ear. You may find out that this complaint could potentially save you from a bigger disaster down the road. Use constructive criticism as just that. Use it to construct a better business module, which in turn will help you build a better and stronger business. We may be the brains of our companies, but the consumers are the lifeblood. With their financial dollars, along with great products and services, they keep the business flowing.

Listen to your employees, if you are so graced to have any. They also can see things from perspectives that may be in your blind spot. With an attentive ear to both inside and outside of your company's media campaigns you are on the launching pad for great social media success.

LEARN TO CHANGE WITH THE SEASONS

A great result to listening is conforming to what you have heard. Your social media should not just be one note. Yes, it should reflect your

Core values and mirror what's on your website and brick-and-mortar store. Your social sites should also consist of changing with the times. You would not put a cassette tape in a CD player nor would you put a VHS tape into a DVD player. Although these different forms of media can all carry the same information, adjusting with the times is necessary to keep your brand relevant. Change is not always bad. You don't have to change your company's message or core values to give your business a facelift. A new color here or there will not diminish your brand but will let your customers know that you are always evolving to bring them something fresh and new.

Don't go crazy for likes

We all want to be love or liked, but I have seen many small companies lose it because other brands may get more likes. This can even be seen on a personal level. People are more driven by likes than the product they offer. Some will go as far as posting things that are inconsistent with their brand just to get likes. Believe me when I say people are watching. Stay consistent. Stay fresh. Stay relevant.

Don't measure the success of your brand by likes. Many companies pay for likes and sometimes what you see is not real. Do not become the company that snaps and put others down because of the responses you may or may not be getting with your brand on social media.

Stay classy and grow at your own organic rate. Taking it step by step will help you appreciate your customers that much more when your 100 likes or followers grow to 500, 1000 and beyond. You know that they are real. They are there because they have seen something in your product or brand worth liking.

Building and growing your brand is a process that won't happen overnight. Many businesses that have experienced rapid growth in the first few months of business begin to experience a decline once all the hoopla dissipates. Then all of it begins to balance out, they then can see who their core customers are and the needs of those customers. After a period of time businesses can see what customers are buying, what drives them to the stores and what they like or dislike about their products. Consistency wins the race, connected with great customer support and a needed product. People can like you today and hate you tomorrow. Finding your loyal customer base should be your concern, not gathering thousands of likes.

The Power of the #Hashtag

It is hard to look at any social media post and not see a hashtag accompanying it. Hashtaging has become so popular, that many sites have been developed to help you use its power. So what is a hashtag?

Hashtag-(on social media sites such as Twitter) is a word or phrase preceded by a hash or pound sign (#) and used to identify messages on a specific topic.

On Twitter, the pound sign (or hash) turns any word or group of words that directly follow it into a searchable link. This allows you to organize content and track discussion topics based on those keywords.

A hashtag is a type of label or metadata tag used on social networks and microblogging services which makes it easier for users to find messages with a specific theme or content. Users create and use hashtags by placing the hash(#) character (or number/pound sign) in front of a word or un-spaced phrase, either in the main text of a message or at the end. Searching for that hashtag will then present each message that has been tagged with it.

For example, on the photo-sharing service Instagram the hashtag #bluesky allows users to find images that have been tagged as containing the sky. Hashtags can be used to collect public opinion on events and ideas at the local, corporate, or world level. For example, searching Twitter for #worldcup2014 returns many tweets from individuals around the globe about the 2014 FIFA World Cup.

Why is this important to me or my business?

1. *Encourage user-generated content.*

2. *Aggregate and showcase the response.*

3. *Connect campaigns.*

4. *Repurpose hashtag-driven content.*

5. *Relate to consumers in real time.*

To find out more on how hashtags can be useful to your business continue reading the connected article http://www.entrepreneur.com/article/232289

Using hashtags in your social media campaigns can help you start or track a personal movement or response to your brand. Hashtags should be uses strategically and not be written in a long sentence form. Quick keywords that will draw attention to your brand or event, that can easily be duplicated or remembered are good strategies to use when creating or using a hashtag. The website Twubs.com lets you register a hashtag and keep a count on when, where and who is using it. Use the power of the hashtag to your advantage to solidify and deliver your company and brands message or product to the world.

BRAND BUILDING FACT:

TWEETS WITH 1 OR 2 HASHTAGS HAVE 21% HIGHER ENGAGEMENT THAN THOSE WITH 3 OR MORE HASHTAGS.

Chapter 5

Expand Your Brand

Now that you have the DNA structure for your brand, and your business is in full swing, it is a good time to start thinking ahead.

Many brands diminish for not expanding their brand. This could be a potential failing point of your business. Most people do not like change. We cringe at it, we don't want to experience anything new at the cost of losing something old with which we are comfortable.

Pulling from the DNA

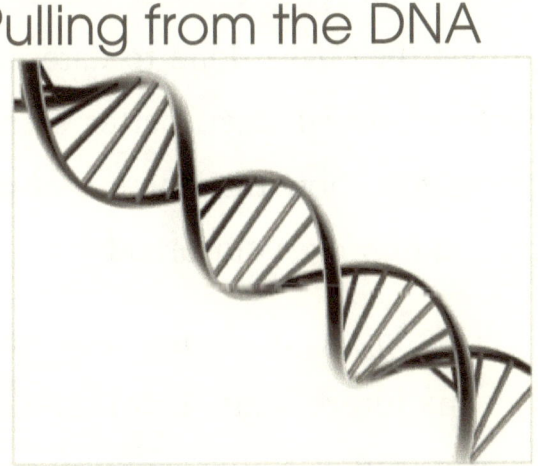

When you know your DNA, you do not have to lose what your consumers expect from you. You can capitalize and grow above what they expect. Pulling from your brands DNA says that this is still a part of what we are doing, but we are always striving to do it better and give our customers a better product.

When you look at larger brands you see this action done all the time. They are consistently adding something new to their products. Take soap for instance. All soaps have the goal to get you clean, but when companies began to add to it, they tell you that this is the new and improved soap. They want you to know this is some of the best things they have done to date. It is stronger than before, lasts longer, better scent, etc. They are letting you know that there is always a way to expand and improve your brand.

Expanding your brand will cause you to think in the future a bit. Think about your brand and what it is now. Now think way into the future about what your brand can be. What are some out of the box uses you could see for your brand? What way can you use this product like never before? What brand would you like to collaborate with to take it even further?

All of these things are possible to do without losing the DNA of your brand. Once you have built a strong brand, it is easy to branch off into things that you may have never thought of.

Look at people who are famous. They may have started out as a singer or a clothing designer.

However, looking at the complete body of their work, some now have perfumes, home decor and a variety of other products connected to their brand. Their brand, as well as your's, demands a certain quality and essence that has to line up with there DNA to produce the same results.

Companies are looking for brands that have strong DNA of proven sales and a cult following. They want to align themselves with those brands to grow stronger and better.

There are many ideas and businesses that can be birthed out of your brand, with a little thinking into the future. It doesn't cost you anything to think intuitively and ponder on different ways to expand your brand. What it can do is give you a growth goal and a great expectation of what you can be.

Many investors will not even bother investing if your business is one tract. They are looking to see your 5-year plan. What is your 10-year plan? If you are good at something certainly keep up with it and don't do away with the formula but, do not get caught in a time warp thinking that there is only one way to do it.

The Evolution of the Sony Walkman

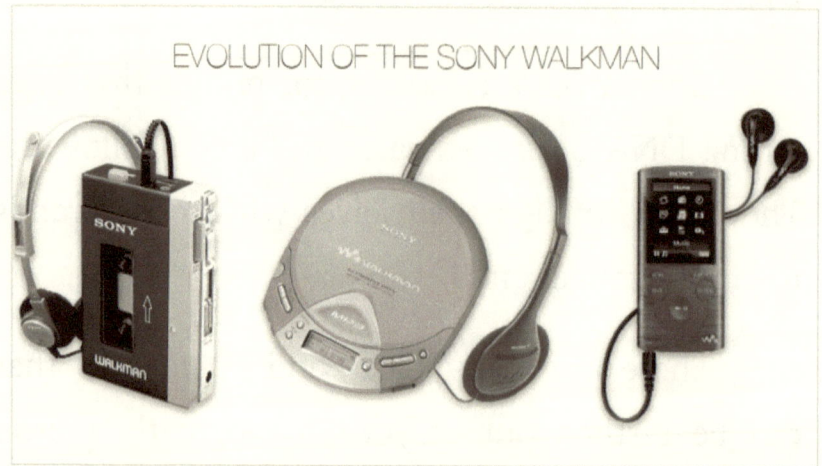

EVOLUTION OF THE SONY WALKMAN

Lets look at something simple. Take the Sony Walkman for instance it made its first debut in July 1979. Then it was the vanguard of technology for a portable listening device. The Sony Walkman TPS-L2, a 14-ounce, blue-and-silver, portable cassette player with chunky buttons, headphones and a leather case. It even had a second earphone jack so that two people could listen in at once. This was something at the time considered to be ground breaking. As time went on, Sony and other portable devices have come to surface and some with considerably successful followings such as the portable CD player, to MP3 players all the way up to now with the iPod touch.

This particular list goes hand-in-hand with many products that we see and use today, from cars to computers, sports, foods, disk drives and the list goes on and on.

Somewhere along the line, someone realized that they could take the technology further and beyond what ordinary people thought its uses could be. Go ahead, think outside of the box, even if the technology of what you're dreaming up has not been created yet. You could be on the ground floor of forefront technology.

Downfalls of not Expanding Your Brand

Lets look at Kodak. The name that is synonymous with photography has now, to some, become an after thought. Believe it or not Kodak was the first to invent the digital camera. The digital camera was invented in 1975 by Steve Sasson, a Kodak engineer. When presenting the idea he characterized the initial corporate response to his invention this way: It was film-less photography, so management's reaction was, "That's cute—but don't tell anyone about it." Wanting to stick to their guns on being the premier film maker, It caused them not to capitalize on what they had to expand the company into new and fresh territory. Kodak could have been the forerunners of a brand new technology. To find out more on Kodak's downfall and resurgence here is a link to find out more about what helped and hurt them.

Expand your brand by expanding your thinking. Aim for the fence and take calculated risks, but take the risks nonetheless. It could be the facelift and the momentum that your brand needs to keep its continuing power and to remain relevant in the forefront of change to an ever-evolving generation.

BRAND BUILDING FACT:

FORTUNE REPORTED THE "TOP REASON" THAT STARTUPS FAIL: "THEY MAKE PRODUCTS NO ONE WANTS." A CAREFUL SURVEY OF FAILED STARTUPS DETERMINED THAT 42% OF THEM IDENTIFIED THE "LACK OF A MARKET NEED FOR THEIR PRODUCT" AS THE SINGLE BIGGEST REASON FOR THEIR FAILURE.

Bye, Bye

Many entrepreneurs are so caught up on what they are building and starting that they don't look to the end. It seems as if it is the last thing that we want to look to. We do not want our baby to end. We don't want to hang up something that we have spent so long and hard a time to create.

This could be the best thing that ever happened to you and your business. Someone else may be able to take your brand to levels that you never imagined or even wanted to deal with. Your company's growth can attract other companies or investors who may want to buy you out.

No one wants to leave the baby they created, and that's understandable. There are many ways that you can exit without leaving your brand cold turkey. You could still be on the board of directors and have someone else deal with the day-to-day task of keeping the ship afloat. You can stay in the creative department and give the direction on where you would like the brand to grow. You could just take the billion dollars they are offering you and just start all over on a new task and adventure. With that kind of money, who couldn't dream of ways to start fresh? You just may want to buy a small island and relax for the rest of your life.

Either way, many owners have stunted the growth of their companies' potential by being so connected with it, that they are afraid to let the baby grow and see what it really can be. Your company or brand may be bigger than you have imagined or could have imagined. You still could be a part of the next best thing that you created.

One thing that I have learned in business is that there is always someone who is a little bit smarter, wiser and stronger than you in any given field. Taking them on as partners or entrusting them to take your brand to new heights is something that should be at least considered to see if it may be a good fit for you and your brand.

Having an exit strategy shows that you have thought ahead. You are willing to take new risks and that you are not afraid to have your business grow exponentially with another investor or professional expertise.

Chapter 6

Fail your way to success

Many people are afraid of failure. Just thinking of the word conjures up thoughts of our biggest fears. In the business world to be successful and maintain a successful business, believe it or not, you have to fail.

Thomas Edison

I haven't failed. I've just found 10,000 ways that won't work. *Thomas Edison*

The above quote is believed to be taken from Edison when trying to find a way to create the light bulb. It is said that he tried over 10,000 various ways to get it to work to no avail. Someone asked him, "Aren't you tired of attempting this seeing you have failed over 10,000 times?" Edison then replied, "I haven't failed. I've just found 10,000 ways that won't work."

Having this entrepreneurial mindset tells life and all of its obstacles there is a way to be successful and there is a solution to every problem. We all need this mindset and must continue to learn from it daily, no matter what we may face. Use every failure as a lesson and every accomplishment as a ladder to climb higher.

We have been taught ever since we were children that failure is a bad thing. It has been so ingrained in some of us that we try to avoid it at all costs. In the business world trying to avoid failure is useless. Failure is part of the cycle to success. Are there avoidable mistakes that should be adverted? Yes. Experiencing failure shouldn't be one of them.

Once you have embarked on the task of doing whatever it takes to become successful, prepare your mind to understand that everything will not work out the way that you think it should, or at all. It is from those bumps in the road that you learn to maneuver and adjust to what lies ahead.

Fear and Failure

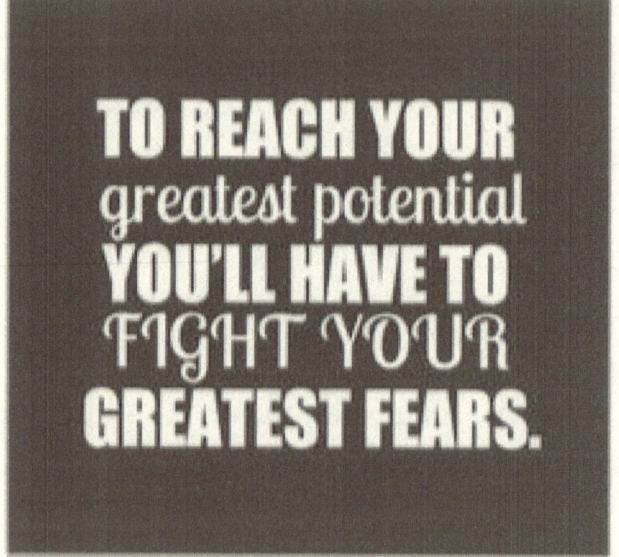

TO REACH YOUR greatest potential YOU'LL HAVE TO FIGHT YOUR GREATEST FEARS.

Failure is often connected to fear. We are afraid that our business will not make it. Afraid that we will lose our investment. Afraid that people won't like or buy your products. These are legitimate thoughts, but they shouldn't be hindering thoughts. When you allow failure to cripple you, you are not just letting it cripple you it has a ripple affect. It will cripple your thought process, your business, and your customers will never get a chance to hear about your products because you were too afraid to step out and give it a shot with all you've got.

Overcoming fear is part of the process to exploring new territory. Your mind needs to be programmed to a new way of life. Although it may constantly tell you if you go too far you will be broke, you will waste your time, this idea will not work, etc. Contrary to that, what if during your success journey you don't go broke and you end up a millionaire or greater. There is just as great a possibility for one as the other. The odds will even be greater in your favor if you don't give up.

Fear has stopped many great ideas and inventions from coming to market and is responsible for the depression of many once hopeful entrepreneurs. When someone else comes out with the idea you had, the same fear that controlled your emotions before, is now taunting you saying you should have gone through with the idea. Letting hard times and fear stop you from going forward, only hinders the development of what you could be if, you had never let fear stop you.

Stepping Stone

Use the different failures in your business as stepping stones. Learn what you can from them. Remember, people can tell you only 3 things yes, no or maybe.

Learn the Ratio

If 5 people say no and one says yes, that one yes could be all you need to keep you going. By not stopping you could acquire 10 more no's and 2 more yes's. You now have developed a ratio to follow. Your ratio will continue to grow the more you fail. Failing gives us lessons on how to perfect our product, pitch, and performance. Learning from your failure gives you the antidote to get a yes from the consistent no's and closed doors of opportunities.

A great place to learn

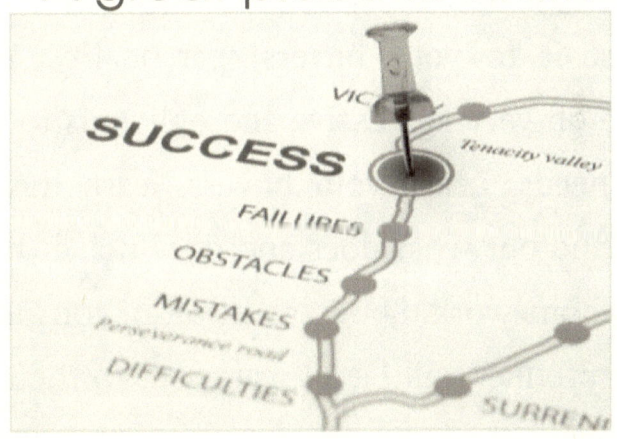

Learn to use failure as fuel. The more fuel you have the further you can go. Often we feel that we fail because we got rejected from one source. This is a great time to learn. If the opportunity is available, ask the potential buyer or client why did they say no. This is valuable information, more than anyone could put in a book and better than any mentor can give you. You are getting information right from the consumer's mouth. Learning to capitalize on this data can substantially convert your rejections into orders.

Learn what the customers liked or disliked. It may be your product. If so, improve it if you're hearing a consistent theme about your product or service. It may be your pitch. If so, learn how to adjust it to your buyers' personality. You may come off very aggressive and oblivious to the buyers' needs. Learn your buyers, learn their habits and find out what does and does not fit them. Do your homework. Show the buyer or consumer how your product will be a great asset to their lives or business.

Every instance of failure oozes with learning opportunity and power to succeed. It is through these failures that your business model is built. Learning what does and does not work saves you the time and resources to focus on what does work and how to perfect and duplicate it.

Do not be afraid to fail. You can never complete your journey or see what the end will be if you give up prematurely.

> **BRAND BUILDING QUOTE:**
>
> MANY OF LIFE'S FAILURES ARE PEOPLE WHO DID NOT REALIZE HOW CLOSE THEY WERE TO SUCCESS WHEN THEY GAVE UP.
>
> THOMAS EDISON

Chapter 7

The Power
Of Perseverance

PEOPLE OFTEN ASK ME, 'HOW DID I GET TO WHERE I AM TODAY?' MY REPLY, I STOP MAKING EXCUSES AND STARTED MAKING MOVES.

-LS

My Story

Many people ask me how I got started. What did I do? Who helped me? They often want to know what tips I can give. I will try to round it all up with the story of how I got started and my journey to where I am now.

When I was about 7 or 8 years old, I knew that I would have my own company. I used to tell my classmates that I was going to sign their paychecks. Crazy, I know but, it was what I felt deep inside of me. I even knew where I was going to be located and had the phone number I wanted, already memorized.

It was during this time in my early entrepreneurial endeavors that I first got into trouble. A couple of friends and I said that we were going to go into business by selling diaries.

We put our money together totaling about $.75. We would then go to the school store to buy 75 sheets of notebook paper at $.01 per sheet. We cut up one piece of the paper into squares staple and glued the sides together and sold them for a quarter. Just one page after we cut it would give us about seven pages for the dairy, not a bad markup in our minds.

So here we are about the third day into our business, we had sold about $1.75 in diaries and we get caught. Someone got caught selling one and told on the rest of us. The next thing I know I'm on my way to my principles office for selling diaries and waiting for my mother to come to school. Not a happy day for me to say the least.

This incident helped me realize that I wanted to have a real business for myself when I got older. It also taught me that I could not become a salesman on the school's time.

A few years later I began to draw people wearing my brand of clothes, shoes and watches. I could just see my emerging empire in my head. I saw myself with my own brand, having employees and changing the world.

Entering high school I was known as they guy who designs shoes and the guy who could draw. Not a bad moniker to have upon entering a new unforeseen and sometimes scary world of high school.

Almost everyday while in class I was drawing. The teacher would be teaching his or her heart out and here I am designing clothes, portraits or whatever I could to pass time quickly.

In high school, shoes were all the rage. Having the best shoes on your feet served as a status symbol. For those of us who could not afford to pay for them all the time, we would either talk about them or draw them. I was on the drawing end. Around this time in my senior year of high school a magazine called KICKS was released. It featured all the designers from different well-known brands and the hottest shoes on the market. In this inaugural issue it showcased Nike designers. I was stoked!

I read that magazine from cover to cover over and over and over, just imagining my dream job as a shoe designer. I thought, what could be better than going to work and designing shoes all day and getting paid for it.

Often, in school, many of my classmates suggested that I should send my shoe designs to Nike to manufacture them. Heck, I didn't know any better so I sent them off and received a polite rejection letter. That did not stop my passion for working for what was then my dream company.

When entering college, I decided to write everyone at Nike whose names they mentioned in the magazine, from the president to the janitor. I didn't care who it was, I just wanted an opportunity to work there. I figured the letters I mailed before I addressed them "To whom it may concern" so, maybe they just sent me the old prewritten response rejection letters. Now, I have names that I can directly send my letters to. It was on!

I remember it like it was yesterday. I was up late one night and said to myself, "I'll just take a shot." Mind you, I had received a half dozen or so rejection letters in the mail already saying, "Thanks" for my submission, but Nike does not solicit designs from outside designers, blah, blah, blah. I wasn't hearing it.

During this time I was working full time in an I.T. department and going to college full-time.

On top of that, with no car and both places were in opposite directions almost 20 miles apart. During this time I would get up at 5 a.m. and leave the house around 6 a.m. and make it to work around 8a.m. After working 8 hours I would ride the train and the bus to the end of the line and then go to school for 3-4 hours at night and all day on Saturday.

This particular day I was up late after a long day of work and school. I decided I was going to write everyone from the magazine. Great idea! Bad time of day to execute it. So, here I am late at night writing everyone and informing them of my passion for footwear design. Saying, I had a great idea that has never been heard of before and whatever else I could think of to get me a shot. The letter was horrible, to say the least. I still have one for reference today. I cringe and grin every time I look at it. The letter was printed in blue ink because the ink in my printer was low and would only print blue and the words were faded. Secondly, I failed to proofread, so the spelling was atrocious. I just quickly glanced over it and told my-self, "Yeah, this is good to go!" Last of all I printed it on beige recycled paper. You know the paper that has all the dots and marks and whatever on the sheet? Yeah, That. It was horrible to say the least. (This is the actual letter)

It was all that I had, along with great passion and hopes of living my dream job. I was not going to let anything stop me. Soon after, letter after letter began to flood in, "We're sorry Mr. Stepter..." From the looks of it, it seemed that my dream job was just that, a dream.

Then, it happened. I remembered getting home one day checking the mailbox, I had a few more rejection letters in the mail, but one of them seemed different. This one felt a little bulkier than the standard rejection letters I was receiving. So I opened it up and lo and behold one of Nike's senior designers had written me back! I could not believe it! He took the time out of his day to write a letter back to me. This really added a log to my fire! Out of all the rejection letters and disappointments going on within, someone had noticed my passion and was willing to give me a shot and mentor me.

From that time on, we kept a correspondence with one another and set up an interview later on that year. He said that he heard the passion in my voice from my letter and felt the need to respond because he was once that kid. In fact he was Nike's first design intern.

I suddenly went from a kid designing shoes to preparing my portfolio for an interview at Nike. To say I was excited would be an understatement. I had the date circled on my calendar: December 3, 1999. Coincidentally, I'm writing this on the same date (not the same year of course). This was going to be a year of firsts. My first plane ride and my first interview with a global company.

I asked my godfather to go on the trip with me to help balance my nerves and for the support. So I flew from Chicago to Minneapolis to pick up my godfather, flew from Minneapolis to St. Louis and from there to Oregon. What a first flight!

So I flew out to Portland and arrived on Nike's campus. To call the campus "amazing" does not begin to describe the campus back then. I went in to where I was instructed to go and waited for the designer that was mentoring me to meet me at the front desk. I was just in awe reflecting in that moment, that I had gone from extremely poorly written letters to Nike's corporate office. I was just like a sponge soaking in the whole experience.

My mentor came down to get me so we could go to his office and chat for a while. I showed him my portfolio and to be honest it wasn't up to par from other submissions they had received. We talked about my portfolio over a time and came to the conclusion that it was not what they were looking for. I received an employee discount and a tour of the office. We then went to lunch and discussed the needed prerequisites to get where I wanted to be in the company. He and the hiring manager gave me some useful information to help me reach the level they were looking for in the internship program, and a load of information to get me started working there. Some of it I can share and other parts I cannot. He introduced me to some of the great minds of our times who have designed shoes for the likes of Michael Jordan and Kobe Bryant to name a few.

Most would say that this was a great failure, but it is in fact a story of triumph. This experience, coupled with perseverance, fear, failure and hope, started the foundational work of the company I have today. Though Nike did not offer me a job, I still have a friendship with that designer today.

It was this experience on the Nike campus that day that ignited the fire in me to start my own company. F.L.A.M.E started from the spark at Nike. I said to myself, "If my determination and passion could get me to this point, imagine what I could do with my own company."

Not saying I wasn't disappointed that I didn't get a chance to work there and fulfill one of my dreams, but the opportunity opened my mind to so much more.

The whole Nike experience is one I will cherish for the rest of my life. Good experience, great people and the birth of my company all came from the passion and perseverance of not giving up.

Some may call it failure. I call it the fuel that ignited part of my purpose. From that spark, my company now has different brands, is expanding and growing at a rapid rate. I now have the privilege of speaking to individuals from all walks of life and can let them know from experience, if I can do it so can you.

In building your brand understand that it will not always be easy. Many things will not work in your favor. The ups and downs come when you least expect them. The joys of business ownership far outweigh the tears and frustration in the beginning stages. Knowing that you are living your passion and will one day share your product with the world will get you through the tough times of brand building and business ownership.

Starting your company and building your brand is an excellent opportunity to live out your dreams. It also gives someone the opportunity to experience the world through your brand and products. Will it be easy? Not at all. Will it be worth it? Sure will!

Chapter 8

Creating A T-shirt Brand

Cuzzo and Beyond

Learning Through Adversity

Around 2006 I had the idea to create a luxury accessory line. I had the name chosen, shared it with a few people to get a feel of what they thought and started the groundwork to create my brand. I began with a few designs made a promotional video and then prepared to get the name trademarked. This began my first dealings with the process and the tedious work and research that it requires to acquire a trademark. I started the search myself through the TESS search engine on the USPTO and thought that I was good. My wife, who was my girlfriend at the time, was preparing to graduate from law school and very interested in practicing in intellectual property. We agreed that she would research the name, prepare and submit the trademark application and figured it would be good experience for her to put on her resume, and would only cost me dinner. It was a win-win situation, so we thought.

We soon received a correspondence letter from the USPTO that there was an office action stopping my trademark application. To our surprise, a company in Australia was using it as the name of their general store. The office action explained that the my name would cause customer confusion with the general store because the general store may sell luxury accessories at some point in the future, even though they only sold nick-nacks and t-shirts currently. The Trademark office gave us the opportunity to give our argument on how our mark would be different. After submitting our rebuttal they reviewed the argument and unfortunately, rejected the trademark application. This is why I explained in earlier chapters that you should acquire your business name ASAP, even if it is just on social media platforms and your websites domain name.

What now?

After experiencing my first hurdle of not being able to continue with that name and company, I took all the lessons learned from that experience and told myself let me learn this business step by step.

The Creation of Cuzzo

CUZZO

I have always created T-shirts as a part of my entrepreneurial quest. I decided to take making tees to a higher level. Considering the experience with my previous luxury line, I thought seriously about a name.

The name Cuzzo was something that was used a lot by myself and others referring to a close friend, buddy or actual cousin who seemed so close that we just called them Cuzzo.

Then I had my aha moment! "Cuzzo"! That's it! It was something that was commonly used by many people and cultures, so branding wouldn't be that hard. It also rolled off the tongue very smoothly.

Next was hoping and praying the trademark had not been registered. After a preliminary search of not finding anything similar, my wife and I again applied for and received the official trademark of the name CUZZO. This was the first step in building my T-shirt brand. To secure the trademark I had to use it in commerce across state lines. No problem, I created a few iron-on tees and was on my way.

After making my first sells I had to gather myself and determine the type of T-shirt I wanted to create. From this thinking, I created a checklist of materials and things needed when creating a T-shirt brand.

Many of you ask me questions on how and what I did to get started. As you have read in my story, you can see it was not easy to get things going. So here is some information, questions, tools and websites to get you started.

- What is the name of your brand?

- Have you acquired the name through a website and social media platforms?

- What is the theme of your brand? Is it Goth? Spiritual? Urban?

- Who is your customer? What are their ages? Where do they live?

- Who will manufacture it? You can have a screen-printer or do the printing yourself with a heat transfer machine. Note: **To take your business seriously, I strongly suggest you do not use iron-on transfers. They are not professional at all.**

- Keep costs low. Find a good quality shirt at a great price. Build a relationship with your printer.

- Use private labeling. Private labeling is you placing your own company's logo and tags on the inside of the shirt.

- Invest in hangtags. This small investment can take your brand from amateur to a real player in the T-shirt game in a matter of seconds.

- Do your best to keep inventory low. It is better to have more demand than supply.

- Charge a premium price for your tees! You put in the hard work and your shirts are worth it. You are in the business to make a profit!

- Do not just give shirts away because people are cool. Remember: You operate a business.

If people really like your brand they will support it with their money as well as with word of mouth.

- If you are going to give away product, do your best to make sure it is an influential person who can bring exposure to your brand.

- Think ahead. Where do you see your brand in the next few years?

- Be prepared to launch when the new season hits. The early bird gets the worms and the sells.

- Check out T-shirt blogs and different sites to see what's in and what you can do to make your product stand out from the rest.

- Stay true to your brand. Many times I wanted to jump into something that was trendy and use a particular designs because everyone was doing it. But it did not reflect my brand and core values. In some cases this is okay, but don't lose your brand identity trying to acquire sales copying everyone else.

- Be prepared to adjust your game plan. I will end this point with a quick lesson that I learned.

During the winter of 2010 when I first released Cuzzo, it was at the end of the era when many were wearing their clothes extremely baggy. This was right before the Euro tailored style became mainstream in the U.S. There I was with a huge inventory of shirts with no one to sell them to. Even the big and tall size guys where trying to get into 2X and 3X tees.

It was then that I devised a strategy to get rid of most of my inventory that was just sitting there. I liquidated everything that was 3X and above and sold it for $5 a shirt. With the liquidated sales revenue I converted my next T-shirt release to smaller sizes.

Even though I may have lost a little bit of the profit from the liquidation, the catch 22 was I was getting tons of advertisement from all the $5 purchases. I was getting calls from all over from people telling me they saw someone somewhere wearing Cuzzo.

Learning how to adjust my game plan in the middle of what could have been an inventory disaster saved my company from having a large amount of stock that would have just sat. Keeping things at a manageable level can help you adjust when you need to make quick moves to keep your brand relevant.

Over the years by following some of the principles and strategies listed above, my company has grown and enabled me to reintroduce my luxury line.

Getting started in the clothing business is a tough task. I advise all entrepreneurs to know your business cost numbers before getting started. Check out the various companies you plan on using to help start and grow your business. Most importantly treat your customers great!

Here is a list of companies and websites that can help you get your T-shirt brand started. As always do your homework before doing business with any company. I do not personally endorse any company, but I would love to get you started in the right direction to shorten your learning curve.

BLANK TEES

1. S&S Activewear https://www.ssactivewear.com
   *You will need a **Resale Tax ID** to receive discounts.

2. Jiffy Shirts http://www.jiffyshirts.com.

3. Sanmar http://www.sanmar.com/index.jsp
   *You will need a **Resale Tax ID** to receive discounts.

4. Royal Apparel http://www.royalapparel.net

5. Next Level Apparel http://www.nextlevelapparel.com/16/home.htm

6. Blank Shirt http://blanktshirt.com

7. American Apparel http://aawholesale.americanapparel.net *You will need a Business License to receive discounts.

SCREEN PRINTERS

1. Art Factory http://www.artfactorytees.com

2. Ooshirts http://www.ooshirts.com

3. Barrel maker printing http://www.barrelmakerprinting.com

4. Custom Ink http://www.customink.com

5. Culture Studio https://culturestudio.net

6. Sharprint http://www.sharprint.com

7. In Your Face Apparel http://www.inyourfaceapparel.com/2/

DESIGNERS

1. F.L.A.M.E Graphic Designs http://www.flamegraphicdesign.com

2. Fiverr https://www.fiverr.com

T-SHIRT WEBSITES AND BLOGS

1. T-shirt magazine http://www.t-shirtmagazineonline.com

2. The shirt list http://www.theshirtlist.com

3. T-shirt forums http://www.t-shirtforums.com

4. T-shirt factory http://blog.tshirt-factory.com

5. Threadless https://www.threadless.com

6. Pop Culture Tees http://popculturetees.com

7. How to start a clothing company http://www.howtostartaclothingcompany.com

ARTWORK FOR YOUR SHIRTS (You or your designer will need a vector program such as Adobe Illustrator to use most of these files.)

1. Freepik http://www.freepik.com

2. All Free Download http://all-free-download.com/free-vectors/

3. Free Vector http://www.freevector.com

4. Vecteezy http://www.vecteezy.com

5. Free Vectors http://www.freevectors.net

6. 1001 Free Downloads http://www.1001free-downloads.com/free-vectors/

7. Free Design File http://freedesignfile.com/category/free-vector/

8. Vectorportal http://www.vectorportal.com

For Brand Consultation Services

(Consultation services to start your branding and questions with your brand)

1. F.L.A.M.E Productions http://www.flamepro-ductions.com/#!building-your-brand/cminz

Chapter 9

Building Your Brand

Recap

Building your brand is not an easy task. With that being said, we will do a quick recap on the essentials for building your brand and starting your business.

Passion

No matter how lucrative your business could possibly be, when starting your company this must be your passion and not just a fly-by-night hobby. It is this passion that will feed you through the lean times and will fuel you for the prosperous periods of success. This is a quintessential necessity when starting your business. This one asset will set you apart from everyone who is just in it for the quick buck. Let your passion dictate your purpose. Fulfill your purpose by living your dream.

Tools

There are different kinds of tools for various jobs. Make sure you use the tools that you need to develop your brand. Set the foundation with your vision board. See where and what you want to be on a daily basis. Let those images of success and financial freedom infiltrate your mind. Let your subconscious thoughts become your conscious actions.

Learn and decide what is the best way for you to fund your business without taking on a significant amount of debt. Make sure you do all of your legal homework. Start your business right from the start so you do not have to play catch up in the future.

Use the power of social media. Most of these tools are available to you for free. Learn to master them. Use those free platforms to bring in revenue. Continue to keep fresh content on your various platforms to keep user interest. Avoid always selling products. Build a relationship with your consumer.

Let your business card and website be a reflection of your brand products and services. Get your services professionally created if possible.

Connect with likeminded individuals who have the same passion and drive as you. Networking with people can connect you to resources that money could never do.

Expand your Brand

Consider the future and envision what you would like your brand to look like in 5 to 10 years. Learn about different avenues that can be connected with your brand to help it grow further than you could have imagined.

Fail your way to success

Never be afraid to fail. It is part of the journey. Failing can give you the possible clues to success. Every successful entrepreneur has had to go this route. In failing, you learn what does and does not work. It also removes the fear of trying. Once that fear is removed nothing can hinder you from reaching your success ceiling.

Persevere

On this sometimes lonely journey to success, there will be times that you want to give up and throw in the towel daily. As explained in my story, I did not let my highs and lows with Nike slow me down. I used it to fuel my future. You must continue to go forward regardless of what you face. Nothing that is worth having will come easy to you. Success will make sure that you pay your dues before it yields its sweet rewards. No matter what, you can make it in building your brand and starting your business.

Build your Brand

Brand building is not for the faint of heart. Many of the world's most loved brands have had to go through the fire to become the powerhouses they are today. Your brand is not different. While building your brand, you will be faced with many obstacles that will grow you and your company. These lessons will then be the secret formula in constructing your success. Successful brands are built on hard work, dedication, and the will to overcome adversities.

It is often said there is a secret to success but, the truth is, there is no secret. The method is going forward when others have given up. Learning the lessons from many who have achieved success and from their mistakes. Having an irrevocable passion about your life's mission and work are all the tools necessary to help you build your brand.

It is my goal with this book and the information provided to give you a path to some of the unanswered questions to start your business and brand building.

As you build your brand remember that it is a reflection of you and will be your image to the world.

I pray much success to everyone of you as you start your business, build your brand and achieve your dreams.